Smart Travel to Egypt

What to See, Do & Eat

Go Beyond the Pyramids, Live Like a Local, Includes a Listing of Budget Hotels & Lodging

By

Jack Waldron

Copyright © 2022 by Galicia Publishing House.

All Rights Reserved.

No part of the book may be reproduced, stored in a retrieval system or transmitted, in any form or by any means, without the prior written authorization of the publisher, except as permitted under the United States Copyright Act of 1976.

While the author and the publisher have made every effort to verify information here, neither the author nor the publisher assumes any responsibility for errors in, omission from or a different interpretation of the subject matter. The reader assumes all responsibility for the use of the information.

GALICIA
PUBLISHING HOUSE

Published by: Galicia Publishing House

Support@BarberryBooks.com

Design & Cover by Angella Sitompul

First Edition

Contents

Introduction 7

Key Facts Overview 12

Egypt and the Middle East: At a Glance 15

    Topography 18

    The Nile 20

    Economy 22

    Population 26

    Religion 28

    Festivals 29

    Education 32

    Food 33

    Movies and Entertainment 48

    Literature 57

    Holidays 58

Essentials for Visiting Egypt 59

    Dress 59

    Money 60

Trains 61

Roads 61

Buses 62

Taxis 63

Car Rentals 64

Carriages 64

Airport to City 64

Security and Law and Order 65

Tourism Companies 67

Budget Hotels 70

    Cairo 71

    Alexandria 74

Places of Interest 76

Nile Cruise 76

Pyramids of Giza 77

The Cairo Museum of Antiquities 79

Luxor Temple and Statues 80

Islamic Cairo 83

Abu Simbel 84

Abydos Temple 86

Aswan 87

St. Catherine Monastery 87

Sharm El-Sheikh and Red Sea Coast 88

Colored Canyon 90

Temple of Kom Ombo and Edfu 90

Cairo Bazaars 92

Coptic Church 94

Step Pyramid (Pyramid of Djoser) 95

Shopping 96

Being in Egypt *103*

Climate 103

Culture: Life in Cairo 105

Cairo Traffic 109

Social Etiquette 114

Hospitality 119

Family Beliefs 120

Arab Honor 121

Social Class 122

Social Meetings 122

Gift Etiquette 123

Business Etiquette and Protocol 123

Important Travel Advice *129*

Do's and Don'ts 129

What to Pack 130

Final Words *136*

Common Phrases in Arabic *138*

Bibliography *153*

Introduction

Egypt is one of the most popular tourist destinations in the world. Owing to its rich history, most people around the world find Egypt a fascinating destination. According to the United Nations World Tourism Organization, it is ranked the second most popular tourist destination in Africa.

In this book, we will be looking at Egypt as a tourist destination for budget travelers. Most of the information in this book will be based on my personal experiences. I have traveled to Egypt two times and continuously stayed in the country for more than 8 months. As a journalist, I have spent so much time in Egypt, gathering data and evidence for documentaries.

My first visit to Egypt was in 2016, which turned out to be a learning tour but also an interesting one. Unfortunately, I ended up spending too much money; I almost hated the country. This was before I became familiar with the country. Once you learn about the city and start interacting with the locals, you realize that you have been spending too much.

In my first two weeks of stay, I spent more money than I used for the following one and a half months. In a nutshell, if you are planning to visit Egypt on a budget, information is key. You should know when to visit, where to stay, the means of transport, attractions to visit, and where to dine. If you do not have a clear understanding of where you will be staying or the destinations to visit, you may end up spending more than necessary.

To help you avoid the mistakes I made during my first visit, I have organized this guide into several categories and subcategories. The guide tries to look at Egypt holistically. If you are going to enjoy your visit and stay in Egypt, you are supposed to start by gathering information. In my introduction section of the book, I mainly look at Egypt as a country. We look at its location, climate, economy, population, culture, and most importantly, history. When you are visiting any new destination, make sure you check out these factors because they determine the ultimate experience of the tour. If you are a regular traveler like me, you can tell how a country feels and looks like just by learning about its background.

The book then looks at the foods and food culture of the country. One of the important aspects of any tourist is food and culture. When you are visiting a new country, you should try as much as possible to sample local cuisines. By understanding how the country cooks its foods, serves the meals, and behaves around the meals, you will find yourself in the good books with the locals. Getting to understand the locals and making friends is an integral part of enjoying any vacation.

The book then goes ahead and looks at the basic infrastructure of the country. Your stay in any foreign country is greatly influenced by infrastructure. Before you travel to any country, look at the transport network, hospitals, schools, and other types of infrastructure. These determine the quality of life and are the ultimate deciders as to whether you will enjoy your stay or not.

The book then looks at the best tourist attractions in Egypt. As a historically rich country, Egypt has endless tourist attractions, especially for those who are geared towards history and religion.

The book outlines all the popular museums and ancient structures you can visit. Most people visit Egypt with the hope of seeing the pyramids. Unfortunately, unless you know how to maneuver the country, you may end up paying heavily to spot the treasured pyramids. The book details where to find all the ancient attractions, how to get there, and the costs.

When you purchase this book, you get more than just information about Egypt. This book is written from first-hand experiences and offers the most practical instructions for any individual visiting Northern Africa country. The book provides detailed information, including phone numbers, emails, websites, and contact information.

Just by reading this guide, you will acquire plenty of contact information that will help you enjoy your stay in Egypt at an affordable cost. The book also provides a summary of tips on how to stay in Egypt peacefully. If you are interested in visiting Egypt, this book provides just the right information that will make your tour more interesting and fun. Read on and enjoy your stay in Egypt.

If you enjoyed this guide, please consider leaving a review online where you purchased this book. Online reviews can help my work reach a wider audience. Thanks in advance.

Now, let's dive into our trip to Egypt.

Key Facts Overview

Name of the country: the Arab Republic of Egypt. 'Misr' in Arabic. Biblical 'Mizraim'

Region: North-East corner of Africa

Official language: Arabic, English, and French, also spoken and understood in urban areas.

Population: 99,413,317 (2018 est.)

Population growth: 2.38% (2018 est.)

Literacy: 82% male and 65.4% female

Religious composition: Sunni and Shia Muslims, Greek Orthodox, Coptic Christians, Jews & Bhai

Currency: E.Pound (LE or EP) (made up of 100 Piasters, coins in a fraction of pound)

Land area: 995,450 sq km (384,345 sq miles)

Time zone: GMT + 2 hours. Summer: GMT + 3 hours.

Telephone: Country code: 20. For dialing out, press 00.

Electricity: 220 volts (50 Hz) (2-pronged plugs)

Climate: Hot: dry summers and mild winters.

Other main cities: Alexandria, Port Said, Suez, Luxor.

Major international airports and airlines: Cairo, Luxor, El Nouzha, Hurghada, Sharm el-Sheikh; more than 40 international airlines fly to Egypt; round trip tickets, on average, as low as $ 650 to $ 800 (New York-Cairo, for example) depending upon the tourist season. Egypt Air operates most internal flights.

Government: Bicameral legislature, President head of state, elected for a 6-year term.

National holiday: National Day, July 23 (1952)

Visa: Required. EU, US, and passport holders of 40 countries are granted a visa on arrival at the airport ($25).

Vaccinations: The CDC and WHO recommend the following vaccinations for Egypt: hepatitis A, hepatitis B, typhoid, yellow fever, rabies, meningitis, polio, MMR, Tdap, chickenpox, shingles, pneumonia, and influenza.

Egypt and the Middle East: At a Glance

If you are planning to visit Egypt, you should be ready to learn some history. Most of the tourist attractions in Egypt are historic, some dating back to 6000 plus years ago. Even if you have not been to Egypt, you have already heard a lot about this desert country. You probably already have a predetermined view of the country.

As one of the countries mostly mentioned in religious books, Egypt has a long-standing history, which makes it even more attractive to tourists. If you are puzzled by archeological formations, and ancient world architecture and find interest in Abrahamic religious teachings, you should definitely visit Egypt. Let us start by looking at the history of Egypt and the current findings that reveal the country's history.

Dating back to 6000 BCE, the Egyptian archaeological finds show the ancient foundation of Egypt when the primitive form of farming along the banks of the Nile existed, the sole agricultural activity that has continued over the centuries as a dominating activity in its economy. Besides, the country has always enjoyed an influential role in the social, cultural, and religious history of the Arab world.

Glossing over the different stages of its history, Greco-Roman empire (332BCE-330 CE), Ptolemaic Egypt (323 – 30 BCE), Roman Egypt (30 BCE – 330 CE), Byzantine Rule (330-642), Islamic Caliphates (642-1517), Ottoman rule (1517-1805) and British rule that came into effect in 1882, it is the modern phase of history which would be of more interest to ordinary tourists. It had a distinct beginning from 1952 when Gamal Abd al-Nasser led a military coup to dethrone monarch King Farouk I and become the President.

A colonel in the Egyptian army, Nasser was the first ethnic Egyptian to rule over Egypt since the pharaonic times. After declaring the country to be a republic, he showed strong nationalistic fervor and removed the British presence in the country. Following the left of the center policies, he launched an ambitious project of industrialization and modernization to transform the country into a progressive entity. He nationalized the Suez Canal in 1956, which was owned by the British and French governments. He became a bitter enemy of Western imperialism, supported the African cause for freedom from colonial powers, became a champion of the Pan-Arab movement, and gained international recognition as the leader of the Non-aligned Movement to protect the interests of the Third World.

The Arab-Israeli war of 1967 was a devastating blow to his leadership. The economy stagnated. Yet, he was regarded as the most popular leader in Egyptian history. Anwar Sadat (1970-81), who took over as President after him, reversed Nasser's socialist policies and introduced an 'open door' policy to encourage investment and liberalized economy. In 1973, his army dealt a military blow to Israel, nudging it to make peace with Egypt. Hosni Mubarak took over after Sadat's assassination in 1981 and became the longest-serving President (1981-2011). He introduced more political reforms and continued economic liberalization leading to impressive growth in the 1990s, though he refrained from playing any leading role in the Arab world.

In 2003, the political unrest against Hosni Mubarak went out of his control. People clamored for democratic reforms and civil liberties. He resigned in February 2011. This created space for Muslim Brotherhood-backed Mohamed Morsi, who gained power for a short duration. It faced stiff opposition from a large segment of people that forced the military to step in. The military leader suspended the constitution and organized parliamentary elections in 2012 under a new dispensation after a public referendum. The military chief Abdel El-Fattah El-Sisi won the election in 2014 and is the current President.

Topography

For anyone intending to visit Egypt, it is important to note that the topography plays an important role in the country's beauty. To start with, Egypt is a country that is known to be a desert. Being a desert country, you should expect plenty of dessert features. With that in mind, the country is home to the world's second-longest river and also has a very long coastline.

The country is also strategically located in the northern part of Africa. It borders the Middle East, Europe but is situated in Africa. This makes it one of the most uniquely located countries in the world.

If you are visiting Egypt from Europe, you won't spend hours on your flight. If you are traveling from the US, you can have a stopover in Europe and pick a short flight to your destination. From Egypt, you can also have quick access to Middle East countries such as Iraq, UAE, and Qatar. Besides, you can also take a quick tour of other Africa countries that border the country, such as Libya, Sudan, or Ethiopia.

Bordering with the Mediterranean Sea in the north, Israel and the Red Sea in the east, Sudan in the south, and Libya in the west, Egypt is in the northeast corner of Africa. Despite its large land area, the country is primarily an uninhabited desert. Over 95 percent of the population lives within a narrow strip of fertile land along the river Nile.

On either side of the Nile lie vast barren, hot and dry deserts. At its eastern edge lie the Red Sea Mountains, with peaks of over 6,500 feet. The Sinai Peninsula, an extension of the Eastern Desert, is a triangular-shaped, sparsely populated area. Several popular tourist resorts have been developed in the coastal peninsula along the Gulf of Aqaba and the Red Sea. On the west of the Nile lies the great desert of Sahara, which has 60 percent of Egypt's total land area – also mostly barren and sandy and harsh with some oases which provide water to sustain small farming communities.

The country can be divided into four regions: (i) The Delta and Nile Valley covering an area of about 14,000 sq miles. The Nile Valley from Cairo to Aswan, a narrow stretch of cultivated land, is 621 sq miles long. (ii) The Western Desert, the largest in the country, is 259,000 sq miles, stretching from the Nile Valley into Libya, and is rich in natural resources. (iii) The Eastern Desert that covers almost a quarter of Egypt's land surface is a barren plateau, indented occasionally by cliffs and mountains on its eastern edge. (iv)The Sinai Peninsula, a triangular wedge to the east of the Suez Canal. Its southern part is mountainous (Mount Sinai), with Mount Catherine, the highest point towering over the desert at 8,667 feet high.

Among the five big cities, Cairo is the capital on the river Nile, with an estimated 20 million inhabitants, followed by Aswan, Luxor, Alexandria, Sharm el-Sheikh. Gaza is an industrial hub. The cities of Port Said and Suez lie on the opposite ends of the Suez Canal.

The Nile

One of the major attractions in Egypt is the Nile River, which is an important part of Egyptian history. You will find the Nile River in all historical records about Egypt. Even today, the Nile is still an important part of the country and is recognized by the UN as the main water source for the northern Africa country.

Interestingly, although the Nile originates in Uganda, the Ugandans and other African countries where the Nile crosses are not allowed to use the water extensively. The water of this river is reserved for the Egyptians, owing to the fact that the country does not have any other source of water.

When you are visiting Egypt, you will learn some interesting facts about the history of this river. You should be ready to get educated on the advanced irrigation systems used by ancient Egyptians and the Romans when they ruled Egypt. You will be wowed by the techniques and technologies used by ancient Egyptians that are yet to be understood in the modern world.

The river Nile is the lifeline of the country. Egypt is, therefore, also called the gift of the Nile. The river has played a vital role in the country's history, economy and culture. The archaeological evidence shows that as early as the tenth millennium BCE, primitive farming along the banks of the Nile was in practice. Though the Nile River Valley was the cradle of ancient Egyptian civilization, approximately 90 percent of present-day Egypt is desert. Less than 10 percent of its land is cultivated or settled. Its population is concentrated in the river's valley and delta.

The Nile river, rising from Ethiopia and Uganda, snakes northward through Sudan to the Mediterranean. Between Sudan and Cairo, the river flows through a river valley lined with cliffs. As it passes through Cairo, it splits into two, creating a delta, a fertile flood plain of silt, and a series of lakes.

The Suez Canal plays a significant role not only in the Egyptian economy but also has a bearing on world trade as well. Ships plying between Asia, Europe, and the Atlantic avoid circumnavigating the African continent. The canal cuts through a 120-mile length between the two points, separating the bulk of Egypt from the Sinai Peninsula. It took 10 years and $ 100 million to build and was opened in 1869. Now, an average of 50 ships navigates the canal daily, carrying more than 300 million tons of goods per year, which roughly represents 8% of the world trade. With the recent widening of the canal from 61 meters to 312 meters, ships can pass in both directions simultaneously. It contributes 30-35% to the Egyptian economy.

Economy

If you are looking to enjoy a budget holiday, you need to keep the factor of a country's economy in mind. The travel destination expenses depend on the status of the economy. In most cases, developed countries with a stable economy will present better living standards at a high cost. On the other hand, less developed countries are usually more affordable. With that in mind, you should remember that less developed countries carry more risks, such as theft and diseases.

In the case of Egypt, it is the perfect travel destination for anyone looking to have fun in a safe place without necessarily breaking the bank. Egypt is not a developed country, but it is a middle-income country that is still developing. This means that you will find the country to have sufficient infrastructure to accommodate travelers. The country is well endowed with transport facilities, medical facilities and enjoys a thriving hospitality industry. Thankfully, being a developing country, the cost of staying in Egypt is relatively affordable as compared to competing tourist destinations in Europe and the Middle East.

Economic growth in Egypt has been held back by a severely limited amount of arable land (less than 5% of the total area) as well as a large growing population. The lack of growth was also due to the dominant role of the state-owned enterprises until Sadat's 'open door' policy changed the economic landscape. The 1991 economic reforms encouraged the greater role of private enterprise. Despite these reforms, Egypt is still considered a poor country. The growing population has been a great strain, especially on natural resources like land and water. The country relies on foreign aid and remittances by its nationals from abroad. After Israel, Egypt is the largest recipient of annual US aid.

The manufacturing sector doesn't contribute substantially to the economy. Main industries are steel, cement, textiles, chemicals, sugar, and cotton, which are concentrated around Cairo, Alexandria, Port Said, and Suez. It also produces petroleum, iron ore, phosphates, salt, manganese, limestone, gypsum, and gold.

Despite the fact that the country is largely a desert area (about 96 percent), agriculture is the mainstay of the economy, contributing 18% to it. The limited arable land is, however, very fertile and is intensively cultivated (usually two, and sometimes three, crops are grown. Agriculture engages one-fourth of the labor force and is supported by a well-spread network of canals, drains, dams and barrages. Among the predominantly commercial crops, cotton occupies an important place. The long-staple cotton from Egypt meets one-third of the world's demand and therefore is a source of sizeable foreign exchange earning. Maize, wheat, beans, sugar cane, rice, potatoes, and citrus fruit are other main produce.

The construction of the Aswan dam in 1970 has been a great boon to the country's agriculture. It helped reclaim more than one million acres of land for farming besides helping to control floodwaters, providing perennial irrigation, fishing, and developing more biological resources.

The country also has reserves of gold and red granite, as well as coal, phosphates, iron, lead, titanium, and salt. To complement its burgeoning petroleum industry, a petroleum pipeline has been built from the Gulf of Suez to the Mediterranean Sea.

Since the 1970s, Egypt has also been a recipient of foreign economic aid, chiefly from the US, European countries, and rich Arab neighbors. However, the inefficient state-run enterprises, the bloated public sector bureaucracy, and large military spending have impeded speedy growth and resulted in inflation, unemployment, a severe trade deficit, and heavy public debt. A series of economic and fiscal reforms undertaken in the 1990s, with support from the International Monetary Fund, appears to have had a positive effect on its economy.

Because of the stability the country has enjoyed and its rich historical and cultural heritage, the tourism sector has become the pillar of the economy. It employs 12% of the workforce and contributes nearly $ 13 billion in revenues, which is 6% of its GNP. The government is mindful of its importance and has taken measures to promote it with business-friendly policies.

Population

The second most populous country in Africa, with 79 million inhabitants, its main ethnic groups comprise Egyptians, Bedouins, and Berbers, accounting for 99.6 percent of the inhabitants. The remaining minority includes people of

Greek, Nubian, Armenian, and other European descent. In Lower Egypt, there are still remnants of the Greek, Roman, and Turkish populations that occupied Egypt throughout history.

Approximately 99 percent of Egypt's population lives in the Nile Valley, as the rest of the country is desert. Almost 43 percent of the population lives in urban areas. The largest city is Cairo. The second-largest city is Alexandria, which also serves as the country's main port.

Roughly 90 percent of the population is Muslim; the majority of Muslims in Egypt belong to the Sunni branch of Islam. The remaining 10 percent are Christians, mainly Coptic Christians. There are a handful of Christians from other denominations, such as Greek Orthodox and various Protestant groups.

The majority of the present-day Egyptians are a mixture of the pre-Muslim population of ancient Egypt and the descendants of the Arabs that ruled over the country in the seventh century. Because of their distinct heritage, Egyptian residents of the Nile Valley look physically different from their Mediterranean neighbors. They have darker skin and are generally stockier.

A large number of ethnic Egyptians live abroad, most often in nearby Arab countries. There is also a small Bedouin population in the desert, working as nomadic herders.

Religion

If you are looking to travel to Egypt for religious purposes, you should be careful not to offend the locals. Egyptian tourists are strictly scrutinized by the officials to ensure that they do not convey any information about the country that may contradict their religious views. As a predominantly Islamic nation, Egypt is not openly receptive to tourists who oppose Islam or those who are seen to be supporting Judaism or Christianity.

If you are a journalist visiting Egypt, you may be barred from taking photos, videos, or any evidence of other religions other than Islam. While it's a fact that Egypt is a very rich history book about religion, you should not expect to find the facts openly displayed for you if you are a Christian or a Jew. The country tries to protect Islam at all costs, and most tourists will find museums with historical evidence pointing back to Islam.

Islam governs all aspects of life in Egypt, and it is extremely rare to find an Egyptian who is openly agnostic or atheist.

Cairo has, therefore, a large number of mosques. In fact, the city has been called 'the city of a thousand mosques.' The old mosques were constructed during the earliest times in Islam, right from the rule of Abbasid, Fatimid, Mamluk, and Ottoman periods. The new mosques have also been built with beautiful architectural designs.

For non-Muslims, it is essential to observe the guidelines for visiting a mosque. Foreigners are, in any case, not permitted to enter mosques during prayer time. One must visit a mosque in modest clothing, no shorts or short-sleeved T-shirts. Women should cover their hair. Loose trousers or long skirts are appropriate. There are separate places for men and women after they have entered the mosque, leaving their shoes behind. One has to sit on the floor. For pregnant women or handicapped persons, chairs can be provided. All the rules of public decorum must be observed.

Festivals

Egypt is a country of many festivals. If you are traveling the country in search of new interesting cultural celebrations, you are in luck. It is important to remember since Egypt is a Muslim majority country, most of its festivals are tied to the Islamic religion. If you are enthusiastic about religion or you are looking to explore the Islamic culture, you will have plenty of fun sampling their food, dances, customs, and laws.

As a religious country, Egypt celebrates Ramadan festivities in a big way. Ramadan is a month of fasting during the daylight hours when Muslims refrain from eating, drinking, smoking, and sex from sunrise until sunset. Throughout the month, Muslims strive to engage in more acts of devotion (such as praying and reading the Qur'an) to atone for their sins and spiritually grow closer to God. For Muslims, Ramadan is a sacred month because they believe it was when God revealed the Qur'an to the Prophet Mohammed (PBUH). In addition to being a time of introspection and spirituality, the holy month is also a time for food, family, and community, shaped by unique customs.

The day in the month of Ramadan begins with a pre-dawn meal before the fasting for the whole day begins. In many Arab countries, a 'night caller' tours the neighborhoods to announce to wake up the faithful and remind them of them for the pre-dawn meal. To add color to the festive month, houses and neighborhoods are decorated most prominently by traditional lanterns ('fanoos') in different shapes and designs. These are no longer used for lighting the places but only for decoration purposes.

At the end of the day, when the fast has to be broken by the evening meal (iftar), a cannon is fired, also called the 'iftar cannon' in Cairo. The first day of Ramadan month is celebrated as Eid al-Fitr, a 3-4 day holiday throughout the Arab world. During the day, the working hours are restricted, and at night, after the end of fasting, more gaiety can be seen in the streets and business centers. The end of the Ramadan month is announced through newspapers and television, depending upon the sighting of the moon. It is a most joyous occasion for the families with new clothes and outfits and an exchange of greetings and gifts.

While non-Muslims may perceive the month of Ramadan is a time of hunger, thirst, and deprivation, to Muslims, this holy month is filled with many joyful customs and rituals as well as a time for spiritual expansion and strengthening of values and community. Due to following the lunar calendar, Muslim festivals do not fall on a fixed date and move by about 11 days every year.

Egypt is home to the largest Christian population in the Arab world, over 10 million, making up ten percent of Egypt's population. Most of these are Orthodox Copts. They celebrate the birth of Jesus Christ on January 7, as in other Orthodox countries. The Coptic festivities during their Christmas are more or less the same as Christian traditions in the West, except they begin a fasting period for 43 days in the run-up to Christmas day when they take vegan food. Christmas day festivities are similar to midnight mass on Christmas Eve, a traditional dish of rice, garlic, and meat soup 'fata.'

There are other national celebrations like Revolution Day (January 25), Armed Forces Day (October 6), Victory Day (December 23), Suez Victory Day (October 24).

Education

The level of education in Egypt is good enough to help any tourist have fun. Egyptians are generally knowledgeable and enlightened people. The population is widely educated, and most people speak English. Although the country largely speaks Arabic, most people understand English as well as other European languages such as French, German, and Spanish. If you do not speak English or Arabic and you intend to visit Egypt, I will advise that you find a translator. Although other European languages are well accepted in the country, you will not easily come across people who can communicate in these languages fluently.

Primary education up to 15 years is free and compulsory. Higher education is free in public colleges. Private colleges are expensive. There are several public and private universities in Egypt, the oldest being Al-Azhar University in Cairo, established in 972 as a center for Arabic literature. Other universities include Ain Shams University and Cairo University, Alexandria University, and the American University. The country has several institutes for arts and music.

Food

Egyptian food is a combination of Arab cuisine. The country boasts of its culinary tradition dating back to 5000 years, the times of pharaohs. It also came under the influence of Greeks, Romans, and Ottomans, as well as the European cuisine of French and Britain. Made with different ingredients, the main Egyptian foods are falafel (ta'ameya), molokhiya soup, shaksouka, fattah, kebda, mahshi, koshary, baba ghanouj, samak, genma and dessert snacks like konafa, lomafa.

Since good dishes are hard to prepare and need a lot of preparation, outside eateries don't come up to that standard. Egyptians, therefore, prefer to eat at home, accustomed to being fed by a mother or a wife, and don't see the point of going out to eat when a perfectly good meal can be enjoyed without leaving the house.

Meat in general is considered a luxury, and the Egyptian diet is geared more heavily towards bread, vegetables, and fruits. Culturally, Egyptian fare is a mixture of ethnicities, a consequence of occupation by other cultures over the millennia. In strict Muslim households throughout the country, alcohol is not allowed. Muslims also do not eat pork because they consider the pig an unclean animal.

While the restaurants catering to the middle-class diners and tourists with a broader range of dishes, there are café's, dining, and street stalls that offer simpler popular dishes to common people. The higher prices in restaurants also include service and taxes, around seventeen percent. The tipping varies from a couple of pounds per head in cheaper places to fifteen percent in high-end restaurants

Common food is inexpensive, as the following budget prices of some items will show. Since there are no fixed prices and these vary in different eating establishments, these should be regarded as indicative:

Budget breakfast: EP 3.50-6.00: Many hotels will include breakfast in the price. Please check local cafes and street stands also for great deals.

Budget lunch: EP 4.40-8.60: As long as you avoid tourist restaurants, you can have a sumptuous meal.

Budget dinner: EP 6 – 13: Even if you want to dine at a café or local restaurant, you can still eat local favorites for very little.

Beer (3.30 bottle): EP 3.50-4.50: One can get a good local beer at small shops if one can't find a good bar.

The main Egyptian dishes:

Koshari: Among the top Egyptian dishes, Koshari is regarded as the national dish of the country. It is prepared after cooking separately rice, lentils (black or brown), chickpeas, and pasta. These are then tossed together and topped with thick tomato sauce, cumin-scented and garlic and fried onions made crunchy. Many people use chili sauce, which they find more delicious and stronger.

Bearah: This green dip is made up of parsley, dill, leek, ground fava beans, spices, green pepper, and fried onions on the top. Served with Egyptian bread and green onions, usually served cold, it is found the perfect lunch meal on a hot day.

Kunafa: It is among the favorite traditional Egyptian desserts - a traditional sweet using shredded Kunafa, baked in a deep tray and filled with cream or creamy cheese in the middle and plenty of syrup added on the top right after it's taken out of the oven.

Bamia: It is the Arabic translation of okra. Essentially a stew prepared with okra, lamb, and tomato. There are variations depending upon the region and the spices available. In many places, beef is substituted for lamb.

Fattah: This dish is widely taken through all the Arab countries and taken by all Egyptians. Essentially, it is a meal prepared for special occasions, a big feast on marriage, iftar, Eid al-Adha. It is made of rice with chunks of lamb meat with crispy bread at the bottom.

Fesikh: Pronounced as 'fisik' is made of salted, fermented, and dried gray mullet fish that is found in the Mediterranean and Red Seas. It is another traditional celebratory dish which people take despite some advisories that it is not good for health.

Ful medames: Especially in the northern cities, ful is a staple food. Prepared as a stew with cooked fava beans and served with vegetable oil, cumin, and optionally with parsley, garlic, onion, and lemon juice; it is taken with bread. In a different variation, it is also taken with chili pepper and other vegetables, herbs, and spices.

Hamam mahshi: Another popular dish, which is prepared by stuffing a pigeon with rice or green wheat and herbs and then grilling it. For vegetarian travelers, it is prepared with baked vegetables like peppers or zucchini, which are also stuffed with rice and aromatic herbs.

Hawawshi: Essentially, it is prepared by filling the flat pitta bread stuffed with minced meat mix and then mixed with spiced with onions, pepper, parsley, and sometimes with chili, and baking it in the oven.

Kebab: One finds kebab in the whole of the Middle East, and it is a relished food. It can be prepared with chunks of chicken or lamb meat. These are marinated in yoghurt or sauce, which can hold the seasoning in place. To marinate, Egyptian use spices like curry powder, turmeric, ground cardamom.

Kamounia: This is made of beef and liver chunks cooked or baked. Sometimes it is prepared as beef and cumin stew or made with offal, like bull genitals.

Kaware: These are cow's trotters, which are often relished with Fattah. As a soup, the trotters are boiled as a broth; the tendons from these are believed to have aphrodisiac properties.

Kersha: Egyptian tripe stew.

Keshak: Essentially a yoghurt based pudding, made with flour, sometimes also seasoned with fried onions and chicken.

Kofta: It is widely popular in the Middle East. It is made of minced meat rolled into finger-shaped pieces that are grilled on charcoal.

Macaroni bechamel: It is a very popular dish. Prepared with rigatoni in silky bechamel sauce and then layered with meat mixed with spices and tomato sauce. A top layer of another creamy bechamel sauce is put before baking it to crusty perfection. Some Egyptians prepare it in Greek pastitsio using Egyptian cheese, gebna rumi, along with a mixture of penne macaroni and bechamel sauce

Mahshi: Because of its origin in the Ottoman empire, Mahshi is a popular dish throughout the Middle East and even in part of Europe. It is stuffed squash with different names; in Egypt called dolma as the main dish and served on celebratory occasions and is both vegetarian and non-vegetarian. It is stuffed with ground meat, onion and tomato puree, and rice in a variety of white zucchini.

Mesaqa'ah: Another popular Egyptian dish, Mesaqa'ah is prepared by slicing eggplants and grilling them before placing them in a flat plan with onions, green and chili peppers. A layer of sauce of tomato paste and spices is put on the top before baking it.

Molokhia: A popular dish, sometimes regarded as the national dish of the country, it is prepared in different styles, though essentially it is a green soup made from minced jute mallow leaves and cooked in broth. The mallow leaves are finely chopped and mixed with garlic, coriander, and aromatic spices.

Mombar: It is sheep fawaregh, a kind of sausage popular in Egypt and large parts of the Middle East. It is prepared from sheep intestines stuffed with a mixture of rice and meat before being deep fried.

Rozz me'ammar: It is regarded as an authentic Egyptian dish since ancient times. It is prepared with cooked white rice, milk, butter or cream, and chicken broth. The ingredients are mixed in a clay pot and served in a clay casserole dish called 'bram.'

Sabanekh: Essentially, it is Egyptian spinach served with rice, sometimes added with a fresh lemon juice that gives it a tangy flavor and pieces of beef.

Sayaidya: It is a popular dish in coastal areas and is prepared with rice and onion cooked with tomato paste and served with sayaidiya fried fish.

Shakshouka: A popular dish in Egypt, Palestine, Morocco, and Tunisia, though the Egyptian's version is quite different and is prepared with eggs mixing it with onion, green pepper, and tomato sauce.

Torly: A nutritious dish of mixed vegetables like squash potatoes, carrots with chunks of beef or lamb baked.

Qolqas: It is prepared with taro root after it is peeled, though not always, and mixed with chard or tomato. Qolqas is taro.

Samak Fish: This fish dish is popular in Egypt and in Lebanon. In Alexandria, Aswan, the Red Sea, and Sinai area, Nile perch, squid, and prawns are bought frozen. These are grilled for serving with salad, lemon slices, mayonnaise, sliced olives.

Desserts: The Egyptian desserts are more or less the same as available in the Mediterranean region. The main is Basboosa, which is of Ottoman origin and is made from semolina and soaked in syrup. Similar to Basboosa is Harissa that is thicker and different in texture and taste; Feteer meshaltet is a pastry that is dipped in honey or is taken with other sweet fillings; baked sweet potato, rice pudding, sweet goulash, and qatayef are other dishes. Of course, baklava is prepared in all the Middle Eastern countries with many layers of phyllo pastry, a mixture of nuts and soaked in sweet syrup. Ghorayiba is a kind of sweet cookie made of flour mixed with butter and sugar with a topping of roasted almonds.

Kahk is another dessert that is most commonly prepared during Eid al-Fitra in Egypt. It is a sweet biscuit that is covered with sugar icing. It is also stuffed with dates, walnuts, or 'agameya' or served plain. Kunafa is a sweet cheese pastry in syrup. Luqmet el qadi are crunchy donuts, round in shape and small in size. These are soft and filled with syrup. These are often served with cinnamon and powdered sugar. During Ramadan, another special sweet prepared is Atayef. It is a kind of mini pancake sweet with cream or nuts. Rozz be laban is white rice cooked with full-cream milk, sugar and dusted with cinnamon powder. Also eaten with ice cream. UImm Ali is a special bread pudding that is served hot.

Restaurants: Most of the restaurants serve popular food like lamb kebab or kofta. These are accompanied by salad and dips and babaghanoug (made of eggplant). Hummus (chickpeas paste) is the most common that goes with salad and meals. The chicken is on the common menu everywhere. Many serve pigeon with spicy wheat filling. In posh restaurants, one can find a pigeon in a tageen or ta'gell that is stewed with tomatoes, onions, and rice in a clay pot. On average, one will get a standard meal in popular restaurants at about EP (Egyptian Pound) 35-50 per head Egyptian Pound. The high-end restaurants prepare a wider variety of mezze, like olives and stuffed vine leaves, soups, and dishes such as molukhiya, mahshi, and torly with lamb or beef.

Ful ('fool') is inexpensive fava beans that are prepared in different styles. It is boiled and mixed with tomatoes, onions, and spices. It is often taken with chopped boiled eggs, especially for breakfast. Sandwiches of ful are also commonly available at street food outlets.

Taamiya (popularly called 'falafel') are fried patties made of green beans that are lightly spiced and served in pitta bread with pickles, salad, normally priced at EP 1-1.50 per piece.

Makarona, another cheap café perennial that is baked into a cake with minced lamb and tomato sauce. It's rather bland but very filling. It is very similar to kushari prepared with a mix of noodles, rice, macaroni, lentils, and onions with spicy tomato sauce, sometimes with garlic. Sold in different portions at EP 5-7.

Fifteer is another commonly available dish at street food outlets or restaurants, sometimes called fatatri. It consists of flaky pastry filled with cheese, egg, onion, and olives, sometimes with raisins, jams, or curds, and costs EP 5-25.

The Egyptian sandwiches are small rolls with basturma (pastrami) or other fillings like cheese, grilled liver, spicy green peppers, onions, sometimes with tiny shrimp or mokh (sheep's brain).

Torshi is a common appetizer, a mixture of pickled radishes, turnips, gherkins, and carrots; luridly colored, it is something of an acquired taste, as are pickled lemons, another favorite.

Shawarma is the most popular dish in the Arab countries. It is prepared with sliced lamb, stuffed into pitta bread, or simply a roll garnished with salad. A street stall will sell it at EP 7. A plate of shawarma in an inexpensive restaurant might cost around EP 10.

Cheese: There are two main types: gibna beyda (white), which tastes like Greek feta, and gibna rumi ("Roman"), a yellow cheese tasting a bit like Edam. For breakfast, restaurants also import processed cheese such as La Vache Qui Rit.

Nut shops (ma'la) are a street perennial, offering all kinds of peanuts (fuul sudani) and edible seeds like pumpkin and watermelon. Egyptians munch chickpeas (hummus) after roasting them and then sugar-coating or salting them. These are bought by weight.

Fruits or fruit juice are available according to the seasons. Winter brings oranges, pomegranates, bananas. In summer, mangoes, melons, peaches, plums, and grapes are plenty in summer. The strawberry season is brief in the spring. The most popular dessert fruit through the Arab world is the date that is harvested in late autumn. Apples are not grown but imported.

Tea: Egypt's national beverage is tea (shai). Invitations to drink tea are part of social life. Traditionally, it is served black and prepared by boiling leaves. Tea thus prepared is called 'shai kushari.' Teabags have appeared in recent times, and many people like to add milk. In warm weather, people also like mint tea, which is refreshing.

Coffee ('ahwa) is Turkish style served generally sweetened mild or syrupy. Some people like it with cardamom. Instant coffee is available in tourist places or in middle-class homes.

'Chaikhana' (tea house) or coffee houses have been traditional places for the common people in most of the Arab world. The Egyptian coffee houses have played a cultural role where people meet, exchange news and views, read poetry, and there is a lively discussion on issues that affect the people. These are usually hole-in-the-wall places where most common people relax and enjoy puffing away waterpipes (sheesha or nargila). Women are seldom visible there, especially if not accompanied by a male partner. In recent times, in elite places, young women less inhibited by traditional practices can also be seen.

Another popular drink, **karkaday,** is popular in the Luxor and Aswan region. It is a deep-red infusion of hibiscus flowers and is refreshing whether taken hot or cold. Some other infusions in coffee houses arehelba (fenugreek), yansoon (aniseed), and irfa (cinnamon).

Sahleb is a thick, creamy drink made from milk thickened with ground orchid root. On cold winter evenings, one might enjoy sahleb with nuts sprinkled on top after mixing it with cinnamon.

Alcohol is sold through restricted outlets, and in the western desert or middle of the country, its sale is prohibited. Alcohol consumption is not prevalent among common people. Climatically, the hot and dry conditions can lead to dehydration, and overindulgence in alcoholic drinks can result in agonizing hangovers.

On the other hand, beer consumption is more widespread. Beer drinking goes back to pharaonic times. Local brand Stella is a light lager (4 percent), Stella is another (ranging from EP 6.50 to 10 in general, but going up to EP 30 in cruise boats or high-end bars. Sakkara, Premium or "export" versions of Stella and Sakkara lager are other brands.

Egyptian wines, produced near Alexandria, include Omar Khayyam (a very dry red), Cru des Ptolémées (a dry white), and Rubis d'Egypte (a rosé). None are especially good, though Obélisque Red Cabernet Sauvignon and Chateau des Rêves are slightly better than most. These retail for about EP 80 a bottle in most restaurants, but more like EP 120 on a cruise boat.

Like other neighboring countries, the street food in Egypt with its unique flavor is popular and affordable to the masses. Not known for any special palate among the Egyptians, but if cooked with the right seasonal ingredients, it is delectable.

A stroll along the Hussein mosque near Khan El-Khaleel bazaar will be an experience of a lively authentic food market running through a warren of narrow medieval streets. One finds vegetarian-stuffed vegetables, including vine leaves, green peppers, cabbage leaves, and white and purple eggplant.

Koshari is the most popular street food. Here, spice merchants mix herbs and spices on the floor of their stalls. The shops fill highly colored pickles into the bags and supply them to the restaurants or street food vendors. The butcher shops are also lined up on the street selling beef, lamb, or sometimes camel meat.

Greengrocers are scattered throughout, with some specializing in one type of vegetable or fruit. One turbaned old man sells lettuce while another may have his place full of watermelons in a neat pyramid. A few lanes branching out from this street have covered markets that sell murals, images of saints, or suras (verses) from the Qur'an.

Intermingled among these shops, there are live bird sellers as well. For the customers who take these home to cook, the shops can kill on the spot chicken, pigeon, or ducks.

Movies and Entertainment

When visiting Egypt, you will probably be interested in enjoying a movie in theaters or in your room. While the country has its own movies, you may not find them interesting, especially if you are used to well developed American or European movies. However, the country is home to many movie theaters in the capital, where you can enjoy your favorite movies.

Movie theaters in Egypt usually sample movies from across the world. Further, you do not have to rely on movie theaters to watch your favorite TV show or movies. If you are residing within the capital, you will have access to cable TV or Wi-Fi, depending on your residence. This means that you can watch your favorite movies or shows on Netflix or TVs from the comfort of your room.

Egypt has enjoyed the reputation of the cultural capital of the Arab world since the 1930s. Movies produced there are watched across the Arab world. The golden age of Egyptian cinema was in the 1940s and 1950s, from which emerged one of Egypt's best cinematic exports – Omar Sharif. In recent years, the Egyptian cinema has lost a bit of quality and has declined noticeably since the 1970s, with poorly developed scripts and recycled themes.

Besides a wide range of movie theaters that are coming up as multiplexes, mainly in the big cities, there are still some middle-range cinema theatres built in the 1940s and 1950s, with high ceilings and balconies, but these are in run-down conditions now. The top rung theatres show Hollywood films with Arabic subtitles.

The Egyptian cinema experience is peppered with audience action. People will talk throughout the film – about the film, about daily business, about anything that comes to mind. Babies may cry, cell phones may ring, and none of this generally bothers other moviegoers. Egyptians are expressive and emotive, even in movie theaters. The lower down the movie theater chain you go, the more interactive the audience becomes. They may shout at the screen in disapproval or scream out plot suggestions to the actors. As the film is being screened, don't be surprised if the lights are switched on mid-sentence, and it is paused. This is the unavoidable break that allows people to visit the restroom and satisfy their nicotine craving. Of course, they have no interest in the credits at the end, and they better get up and start leaving. It is all part of the entertainment.

Traditionally, Egyptian films and music are very popular in the whole Arab region. It has a thriving film industry. The films cater to popular family entertainment. With the arrival of Arabic satellite television broadcasters like al-Jazeera and al-Arabiya TV, the state censorship is relaxed now.

Egypt continues to be the home to the largest Arabic publishing houses, mainly in Cairo. However, the press and the publishing industry were overseen by the government until the introduction of the multiparty system in 1977. The three main national newspapers are: 'Al Ahram,' Al Akhbar,' 'Al Gokohouria' and Al Misry el Youm. Egyptian press is influential not only within the country but beyond its frontiers.

Belly dancing, known as 'Ra's Baladi (local dancing), the sexy

Middle Eastern dance, is a centuries-old art form that has long thrived on sensual intrigue. Some historians believe that it was once a fertility ritual, consisting of circular hip and arm movements that mimic the emotions and rhythm of the music. During the Second World War, German spies mingled with British officers at Madam Badia's cabaret; in the 1970s, dancers performed for the American presidents

Egyptians have, however, a conflicted view with this dancing style, some see it as a form of art, but others see it as racy entertainment or an excuse for moral grandstanding.

Foreigners have dominated the belly-dancing scene in recent years — Americans, Britons, and Brazilians, but more especially the other foreigners, especially from East Europe, have made their presence felt and attract a large audience because of the high-energy, athletic sensibility they bring to their performance, sometimes presenting it in overly sexual style. Theirs is in distinct contrast to the subtly suggestive style of the classical Egyptian dancers.

In recent years, one has seen moves to prevent the foreign belly dancers from competing with the native dancers. A top Egyptian belly dancer may command around $ 3145 per performance, which the foreigner dancers undercut.

Belly dance is a traditional item at weddings or such celebratory events. There are training schools to groom prospective dancers in this form of dance.

Besides movies, every tourist is on the lookout for various forms of entertainment. If you are out for drinking, partying, and romantic adventures, Egypt isn't probably the ideal destination. Egypt is predominantly a Muslim country, and most locals tend to be conservative in their escapades. If you are visiting this country, you should try to be respectful to women and men all alike; otherwise, you might find yourself on the wrong side of the divide. With that said, those visiting Egypt can still enjoy entertaining activities such as drinking and partying to some extent. The main forms of entertainment in Egypt include night clubs, bars, coffee shops, casinos, and restaurants.

Nightclubs in Egypt are not many as they are mostly purposed to serve tourists. They are mostly located in major hotels, where most tourists stay during visits. Cairo, the Capital of Egypt, is home to the largest and most popular clubs. Most clubs are found around the Zamalek district, which forms the most entertaining section of the entire city. You may also enjoy night club experiences at the Red sea tourist resort towns of Sharm el-Sheikh and Dahab.

Bars are also available in Egypt and provide entertainment to locals who prefer drinking. With that said, drinking is not popular in the country. For this reason, the government requires that all bars are set up indoors. The country welcomes many styles of beer, both local and international. The popular local drink is Stella, which goes for about 30LE ($5.02) per larger bottle.

The other type of entertainment you will find around is gambling. For those who love gambling, you may enjoy playing your favorite casino games in most towns in the country. Just like nightclubs, most casinos are found within major hotels and resorts.

The most popular nightlife activity in Egypt is visiting coffee shops. As already mentioned above, people in Egypt prefer staying at home with their families. If they have to go out, families go out together to take coffee or tea in coffee shops. The shops also sell sheesha and water pipes. Some local style shops are designed for men alone, while those in uptown areas allow women. If you are a lady touring Egypt, only stick to bars, clubs, or coffee shops in popular uptown regions.

Locals in Egypt do not as much love eating in restaurants, but they offer a good entertainment option. Since ladies are sometimes prohibited from clubs and bars, the ideal place for the whole family to gather is within restaurants. With that said, most Egyptians prefer cooking at home to eating in restaurants.

The other important aspect of entertainment for most tourists is dating. When it comes to social interactions, the Egyptians have an interesting social dynamic. The cities are mostly relaxed at night with some female-male segregation. However, if you want to have fun or find a date in the country, you may still try your luck.

Foreigners are allowed to go out at night with their women and age group of friends. In some nightclubs, you may not be allowed to get in if you are single. Egypt is a country that respects marriage, and most laws and rules are geared towards protecting the institution of marriage.

With that said, it is not all dull and gloomy. As a matter of fact, the country is very entertaining if you love staying in a relaxed environment. As mentioned above, they also have their local dances. There are plenty of clubs that play local music. However, if you are out to enjoy some western music, visit clubs that are situated uptown. They play some amazing western music, including hip-hop and trance.

Most clubs in Cairo and other parts of the country have

dancing floors. As we have seen, belly dancing is the most popular type of dance, which means that clubs need to have sufficient space for everyone interested in dancing.

You can find love anywhere you go in the world. Egypt is definitely not an exception. For men interested in dating the locals, you are in luck. Egypt is home to some of the most beautiful women in the world. Unfortunately, you may not be able to see their face since their dressing code calls for covering the entire body. If you are a good man looking to marry an Egyptian girl, just ask her out. If you are in agreement, talk to her parents, convert to Islam if you are not one, and start the marriage process. Well, it does not sound easy, but that is the only option if you are going to date an Egyptian woman. You cannot indulge in casual relations with Egyptian ladies. You may be allowed to date one for marriage but nothing less.

If you are a lady looking to find love in Egypt, you may not have as much trouble as it is for men. You can go out on a date with an Egyptian man at any time, as long as you like him, and you are willing to conform to his religious beliefs. With that said, western women do not enjoy dating Egyptian men. Most women who have had experiences with Egyptian men say they are rough. Well, if you have lived in the US and Egypt like me, you may understand why they think Egyptian men are rough. In Egyptian culture, men are superior to women, and women are expected to be submissive to men. When an Egyptian man dates a western lady who wants to be equal to a man in all aspects, things can get out of hand. If you are going to date an Egyptian man, you should be ready to submit to him entirely.

With that in mind, you may also find your soulmate in Egypt among the many tourists who visit the country. If you are staying within tourist hotels, you will probably come across plenty of other tourists from across the world. Do not be surprised if you find your next neighbor in the desert country.

If you are going to enjoy sexual intimacy in Egypt, you should keep in mind the facts that the country has strict laws concerning sexual intimacies outside marriage. Premarital sex is illegal, especially if you are dating a local Muslim girl. Abortion is illegal but can be performed at some health facilities. Most importantly, contraceptives such as condoms and emergency pills are hard to come by. You may not be able to purchase any of these from a local pharmacy, and it is always recommended to pack yours before you leave for the trip.

Literature

Egyptian novelists, poets, and writers have had a great influential role in Egyptian society, having produced some of the outstanding works of Arabic literature. The writings of Nobel Laureate Naguib Mahfouz are famous throughout the Arab world. As the largest Arabic-speaking country, Egypt has led the Arab world in academic and cultural life. Historically, Egyptian have prided themselves on pioneering political, social, or cultural movements that spread to other countries. Whether it was the pan-Arab nationalism of the 1950s and 1960s or the modern Islamist movement, Egypt's initiatives have influenced the trend in other Arab countries. Egyptian institutions of learning, especially the al-Azhar university, played the most prominent role in Arab literature and scholarly studies. An average Egyptian would claim to the rightful heir or distant descendant of its ancient civilizational legacy.

Apart from novels, stories, and plays, Egyptian's love for poetry is highly regarded in Arabic literature. Major newspapers routinely review new poems, which attract a wider readership.

Holidays

Since Egypt is a Muslim country, most of the holidays are related to the Islamic religion. These include Eid-al-Fitr, which signifies the end of Ramadan and includes the giving of alms and feasting. There is also Eid-al-Adha, which is in observance of the Prophet Abraham. This celebration entails the slaughter of a goat or sheep. Among the non-religious holidays are Revolution Day (July 23), which honors the establishment of the republic, Armed Forces Day (October 6), Suez Victory Day (October 24), Victory Day (December 23).

The Coptic Christian population celebrates Christmas on January 7 because it follows the Julian calendar. The country's Muslims and Christians also celebrate many folk festivals.

Essentials for Visiting Egypt

Dress

Essentially a traditional society with dominating religious customs, any dress exposing parts of the body might be frowned upon, like shorts or sleeveless tops. This applies both to men and women. Women need to take note of the need to cover cleavage and should not prefer tight-fitting attire. Long flowing skirts or maxi-dresses would be ideal. Additionally, a headscarf/wrap or light cardigan to cover shoulders would be useful. The head should be covered when entering a mosque.

As for walking, though sandals are worn by native women, for visiting tourists, comfortable shoes would be more practical in view of the street conditions, like uneven footpaths and absence of cleanliness. Sandals are also acceptable. One will be required to remove shoes whenever entering a place of Islamic worship.

Money

Firstly, money bills are generally greasy and smelly due to frequent use; hand sanitizer will, therefore, be useful. Secondly, always carry small denomination notes and coins when venturing out. The practice of tips, called 'baksheesh' is widely prevalent. For any service, whether taxi drivers, porters, waiters, or those providing toilet paper in public restrooms, or anyone helping you to load or unload baggage, will expect it.

Tourists are reminded of the presence of scammers. One might encounter them right after getting off the plane.

As in other tourist places in the Middle East, one would come across many who would offer unsolicited assistance or tips for transport or shopping. Usually, they'd claim to escort you to a known shop of their cousin or offer their services as the best guide in consideration of reasonable tip, or 'baksheesh.' It would be safer just to ignore them with thanks. Many tours suggested by them are overpriced. The safer way is to travel in a group to eliminate such traps.

Trains

The train station for going to Luxor is Giza. Many trains leave from Ramses station also. There are 3 classes: Express, Ordinary, and Local. Express trains are comfortable and less crowded. Delays are not uncommon. The main routes which have more frequency of trains are Cairo-Alexandria, Cairo-Luxor, and Luxor-Aswan. The Cairo-Luxor-Aswan trains are run by Watania. Train bookings can be made online. Other mainline trains are run by the Egyptian railways. Direct trains are airconditioned and have first-class coaches, mainly used by tourists and affluent Egyptians. Cairo-Luxor (313 miles) airconditioned compartment for two costs $110, single $80, and takes nearly 12 hrs.

Roads

There is a good network of roads that connects the major cities. The road conditions in non-urban areas may not be in good conditions, rutted, or with disintegrated patches. The secondary roads are not bad, but one would find them with loose sand, mud, or gravel. Due to the flat terrain, the long road travel is in straight stretches.

Driving through the rural areas, one should be on the constant lookout for speed bumps illegally laid across the road by the locals. These can damage the suspension of the vehicle. Driving outside Cairo, one will find police checkposts demanding documents like passport and license.

Buses

For public transport in Cairo, people use trams and buses operated by government transport companies. The services are frequent between 05.30 a.m. until 01.00 at night. However, overcrowding is an irritant, especially during the rush hours when even standing space is difficult. The route and the name of the destination are displayed in Arabic on the front. The conductor (kumsari) collects the fare inside the bus. Smoking is not permitted.

There are inter-city services, but no direct bus service between Cairo and Luxor; it's via Hurghada, time-consuming, and is not advisable for the tourists. The long-distance services are provided by five companies serving their respective sectors. Eastern Delta serves the Canal area, Mansurah, and Damietta; Middle Delta to Kafr al-Shaykh and Manufiyyah, Tanta; Western Delta to Damanhur, Alexandria; and Sinai Bus Company serves Sinai areas. These companies have their offices in Cairo.

The bus services are of three types. First, those calling at every station in the inter-city with fewer stops. Or the express class, offering better comfort, like a reserved seat, cleaner toilet, and snacks. The deluxe class has air-conditioning, but others play with open windows that can let in a lot of dust.

Taxis

Hailed by calling 'taksi' with a raised hand, these are in the main cities. The fare meter is at the front of the dashboard and runs as per the rate approved by the government. The approved fare is also applicable to travel outside Cairo city. In the city, a limousine 'Misr' service is also operated by the government company round the clock. A little more expensive but more reliable, it can be contacted by telephone on Cairo number 2599813. It will also provide a service to take the visitor outside Cairo.

Car Rentals

These can be hired through the hotel or the tourist agencies; the tariff depends on the type of car. An International Driving License is valid for six months.

Carriages

Carriages are a delightful way of seeing the provincial cities and visiting outlying areas. Their ranks are usually found close to the station, and the drivers often know the area better than the taxi-drivers; another advantage is that although slower, they can often travel where the taxi cannot.

Airport to City

The general white and yellow taxis have fare meters while many others run on fixed routes and fares. It is always advisable to check from the hotel the fair amount you should pay for a cab ride and set the fare before getting into it. As a guide, a 3-km cab ride in Cairo could be between EP 2.50 – 3.00. There are shuttle services between the airport and the city with fares ranging between EP 25 and 100; between 65 and 470 for the "limousine services," which are like taxis but with fixed prices depending on your destination and the level of comfort you desire. The public bus service from the airport to the city center has a fixed fare of Piaster 70. The metro ride within the city is most reasonable at Piasters 20–50.

Uber services started in Cairo and Alexandria a few years back. These have become popular and are likely to expand to other cities. Cairo alone boasts of more than 90,000 Uber drivers.

Security and Law and Order

Despite reports of terrorism in the neighboring countries, Egypt has enjoyed relative peace and stability for years. In the past, there have been terrorist attacks against the tourists; the main ones are the 1993 explosion on a tourist bus at Giza Pyramids, the 1993 killing of American and French tourists in Cairo, the 1997 Luxor massacre killing 62 tourists, the 2004 bombing of French flight that ferried French tourists from Sharm El-Sheikh and the 2004 bombings at tourist hotels in Sinai. Though the government has introduced security measures, the tourists need to take normal precautions like not venturing out at night in far-away places, especially in the desert. The American and British travel advisories say 'no' to travel to North Sinai and only essential travel to South Sinai. Tourist places like Sharm

El Sheikh are safer.

Apart from terrorist violence, Egypt experienced significant political turmoil since 2011, affecting the domestic environment. This has sometimes involved violent protests and disturbances, which have resulted in a number of deaths.

Protests, marches, and demonstrations have occurred across Egypt in the recent past. If you become aware of any nearby protests, marches, or demonstrations, you should move away from the immediate area as the atmosphere could change quickly and without warning. Police have previously used water cannons, tear gas, birdshot, and live ammunition for crowd control.

Foreigners engaging in any form of political activity or activities critical of the government may be at risk of detention.

Road accidents are common because of the poor road conditions and traffic rule violations, and, of course, unsafe driving. It would be safer to avoid road travel at night, especially outside the main cities and resorts. Make sure you have adequate insurance.

If you are traveling off-road, employ a qualified guide and obtain appropriate permits from the Ministry of Interior. A tourist police permit is required for foreigners heading south from Nuweiba towards Abu Ghaloum and also east to the Coloured Canyon, and obviously for other specific areas of Egypt.

The crime rate in Egypt is generally low, but over the years, visitors have sometimes suffered armed robberies, muggings (including in taxis), sexual assaults, and break-ins to accommodation and cars. Beware of pickpockets and bag snatchers too.

Tourism Companies

Intrepid: (https://www.intrepridtravel.com) It operates tours ranging between one and two weeks. The two-week tour covers most of the country using a bus, boat, and train, starting with USD 1300. It also undertakes tour packages for neighboring countries like Israel, Palestine, and Jordan.

Memphis Tours: (https://www.memphistours.com) An old company offers a variety of packages, from one day or half-day tours in Cairo or Alexandria to camel-riding trips from Sharm el-Sheikh ($35-90 per head). Their tours also include cruises on the Nile, Lake Nasser, Luxor-Aswan trip along the Nile (from $ 500 per person for a 4-day trip). They also organize tour packages for groups for main sites in Cairo and Luxor. Price per person from $ 1100, depending upon the activities.

Look at Egypt Tours:
(https://www.lookategypttours.com) It runs a variety of day trips that include Cairo, Alexandria, Luxor, and Sharm el-Sheikh, price from $50 and $ 150 depending on the placers to be visited and the size of the group. Longer trips ranging from 8 to 10 days can cost $1500-2000 with meals, guides, and transport. Specialized trips like two-week archaeological tours are popular with those interested in the country's prehistoric times.

On the Go Tours: (https://www.onthegotours.com) Another reputed tourist company, it offers trips within Egypt and to several neighboring countries. Its Cairo to Luxor eight-day trip offers good value from $ 400, like a visit to the Pyramids of Giza, Egyptian Museum in Cairo, temples at Luxor, felucca cruise on the Nile, visit to the Valley of the Kings. It arranges budget lodgings and is a good option for backpackers.

Jakada Tours: (https://jakadatoursegypt.com)

Comparatively smaller agency, it offers trips lasting between a week and ten days, costing $ 600-1000. It has a pool of competent tour guides.

Exodus Travels: (https://exodustravels.com) Offers a nine-day Nile cruise from Luxor, which is a good compromise between luxury and price (around $1,400 per head, all-inclusive), for a group of twenty passengers. Like other tour operators, it also runs a longer trip of two weeks, covering key sights like the Valley of the Kings and Alexandria. The price starts at $ 2000 per person.

Beyond the Nile Tours: (https://beyondtheniletours.com) It runs three tours, ranging from eight to fifteen days with a flexible choice of activities, e.g., balloon ride over the Pyramids ($100) and other optional trips. The long tours begin from Cairo, flying to Luxor and cruise on the Nile, taking one to the Valley of Kings and other places. Relaxing at a Red Sea resort is another option. Prices range from $ 1200 to $ 1400 per person, depending upon the activities.

Continental Tours: (https://www.continentaltours.com) A 30-year old company, it has established a wide-scale network for domestic and international tourist packagers. Located at Isis Bldg., 7 Latin America St, opp. US Embassy,

Garden City.

Budget Hotels

Most hotels have shown the price for a double room, which might change according to the seasons.

One can visit Hostelworld to look for the largest inventory of hostel accommodation. Budget travelers also use Booking.com to find the cheapest rates for guesthouses and hotels.

Finding a hotel without a reservation may not be a problem, but reserving one for the first night will be convenient.

Many hotels provide airport pick up, free, or if the stay is more than 2 nights.

Rooms may not be spacious enough to fit an extra crib for babies.

The budget hostels offer bare facilities, some on a sharing basis, all under $20 per night. In Cairo, some of these are Wake Up Cairo, Freedom Hostel, Dahab Hostel, Cecilia Hostel, One Season, King Tut Hostel.

Cairo

The Best View Pyramids Hotel, Giza district, 1050 meters from Giza Pyramid,

13 Gamal Abd Nasser Street, Nazlet El Samman, Al Haram, Giza, Eg, Cairo, $50 with breakfast.

Pyramids Village Inn (Dr. Eglal Mohamed St, Cairo), 1.2 km from the Giza Pyramids and a 40-minute drive from the airport, $45 with breakfast.

Atlas International Hotel, located within 25 minutes walking distance from Al-Azhar Park, at 2 Mohamed Roushdi St, 25 minute-walk from Al-Azhar Park. $37

Pyramids Eyes Hotel, near Dokki metro station, $57 with breakfast.

Pearl Hotel, Maadi, located near The District Mall, 32 Rd,7 Intersection of Rd.82, offers 48 rooms with sea views, $69 with breakfast.

The Central Paris Hostel, 5 Talaat Harb St, offers a golf course, $62 with breakfast.

Maskadi Pyramids View, 28 Gamal Abd El Nasir Nazlet

Alsman, Giza District, near Meidum Pyramid, $28.

The 3-star Great Pyramid Inn in Giza district, 14 Abou Al Hool Al Seiaji Pyramids Plateau, $68 with breakfast.

Milano Hotel, 2-star, in Dokki district, $ 43 with breakfast, a few minutes' walk from Nasser underground station.

Miami Cairo Hostel, 34 Talaat Harb St, near Egyptian Museum, $ 24.

Grand Palace Hotel, 14 Champollion Rd, 1.7 km from Islamic Art Museum, $ 37.

Sufi Pyramids Inn, 19 Abou Al Hool Al Seiahi St, Giza, $ 39Cairo,

Giza Pyramids Inn, 6 Sphinx St, Pyramids Giza, $ 61 with breakfast.

Nour Hostel, 34 Talaat Hzab St., Dokki district, 20-minute walking distance from Cairo Tower, $27 with breakfast.

New City Hotel, 5 Taalat Harb St, Tahrir Sq, Dokki district, close to Tahrir Square, $34.

Victoria Hotel, 66, El Gomhoria St, near Cairo Ramses

Station, $36.

Tahrir Plaza, close to Liberation Square, Tahrir Square, 19 Meret Basha St. $57.

Sunshine Pyramids View Hotel, Nazlet El Semman, Gamal Abfd El Abd El Nasr St, $ 27.

Marvel Stone Hotel, 6 Gerier St, Nazlet El Semman, Giza, $ 61 with breakfast.

Abdeen Palace Hotel, 2 Sabry Abo Alam St, downtown Cairo, $ 35.

Cairo Paradise Hotel, 41 Sherif St, Al Fawalah, Abdeen (tel:20-2-23964220) $15-20.

Cairo Moon, 28 Adly Street, Bab Al Louq, Abdeen, (tel:20-2-23905119) $20.

23.Cairo Inn, 6 Talaat Harb Square, downtown Cairo, (tel:+20-100-077-3210) $30.

24.Cairo View, 44 A Talaat Harb St, Downtown Cairo, (tel: +20 100 801 64426), $20.

Alexandria

Semirames Hotel, El-Gaish Rd, Al Mesallah Sharq, Al Attarin (tel: 20-3-48468370) $20.

Green Plaza Inn (5 stars), Alexandria Governorate, (tel: 20-3-3830284) $35-40.

Alexander the Great Hotel, 5 Oskofia St, besides the Greek Church, $30.

Royal Crown Hotel, 159 Cornish Road, Cleopatra, Alexandria, $25.

Kaoud Sporting Hotel (Families Only), Geish Road 133, Alexandria, $10.

Luxor:

Cleopatra Hotel, $15-20 (3 star), Gezirat West Bank, Al Bairat (tel: 20-100-386 8345)
http://www.cleopatrahotelluxor.com

Grand Hotel, $10-15, 11 minutes from Luxor Temple. (tel: 20-100-496-1848).

Ibrotel Luxor, $40 (4 stars), Khaled Ibn El Waleed Street.

Gaddis Hotel, $25, (2 stars), Khaled Ibn El Walid St.

Mercure Luxor Karnak, $38 to 45 depending upon rooms, with breakfast, (4 stars), 3 km from the open-air museum.

New Memnon Hotel, $35-40,
www.newmemnonhotel.com

Gold Ibis Hotel, $20 (3 stars), Colossi of Memnon, Luxor West (tel: 20-95-2060984)

Rezeiky Hotel & Camp, $20 (3 stars), between Luxor Temple and Karnak Temple.

Pyramids of Luxor, $15-20 (3 stars) West Bank, Gezira Ramla Nile St.

Places of Interest

Nile Cruise

Nile cruise is a good experience to see the country and the ancient cities on its banks. The Nile is 930 miles long, though the cruise packages do not cover the whole distance. October to April is the best time for the cruise. It should be avoided during summer (June-Aug). There are a variety of cruise packages from two to seven nights with five-star luxuries, the price ranging from $350 to 2000. Usually, slacks, shorts, and t-shirts are fine for dressing, preferable in a breathable fabric, though, during the dinners, a bare shoulder dress will also do. The expected tip could range between $3 and 5 per person per night, which can be left in an envelope at the reception at the end. The short cruises in 'felucca,' the traditional wooden sailing boats are also popular. The price is always negotiable.

Pyramids of Giza

The last surviving Seven Wonders of the Ancient World, these are one of the world's most recognizable landmarks, on the outskirts of Cairo (10 miles). The Giza pyramids were primarily built as tombs for the Pharaoh kings and were under the guard of Sphinx. The whole complex has drawn the interest of travelers from other countries. As in other historical sites, the pyramids have their own stories, but the archaeologists for centuries still wonder how precisely these were built. For tourists from around the world, these continue to be at an enormous scale. One can enter the three Pyramids of Khufu, Khafre, and Memkaure after paying the admission fee.

Great Sphinx of Giza, a colossal limestone statue of a recumbent sphinx located in Giza, that likely dates from the reign of King Khafre (c. 2575–c. 2465 BCE) and depicts his face, one of Egypt's most famous landmarks and is arguably the best-known example of sphinx art.

The Great Sphinx is rated among the largest architectural monuments at 240 feet long and 66 feet in height. Its lion's body and a human head wearing a royal headdress is a single piece of limestone. The pigment residue on its points shows that it was painted. The construction of this wonder is estimated to have taken a hundred workers nearly three years using medieval hammers of stone and copper chisels.

The body of a lion and the head of a human represents a popular mythological figure mentioned in the Egyptian, Asian, and Greek scriptures. This creature, with a pharaoh headdress, was often depicted in ancient Egyptian stories as a male spiritual guardian.

The archeological findings reveal that Sphinx was buried in sand up to its shoulders. It was in the early 1800s when Giovanni Battista Caiglia, an Italian explorer, attempted to dig out the statue. The efforts backed by a 160-member team did not succeed. In the late 1930s, Selim Hassan, an Egyptian archaeologist, finally dug out the statue from its sandy tomb.

In modern times, the Sphinx has continued deteriorating due to natural causes like wind and humidity. The increasing pollution is the latest culprit taking its toll on it.

The Cairo Museum of Antiquities

It has the richest collections of Egyptian past, dating back to the Pharaonic times. Among the priceless pieces of historical exhibits are over 120,000 artifacts, many are not yet labeled and not much in chronological order, yet the visitors get a glimpse of Egypt's glorious past.

Mummies, sarcophagi, pottery, jewelry, and of course, King Tutankhamen's treasures - it's all there. The boy-king's death-mask, discovered in its tomb, is made of solid gold and it has been described as the most beautiful object ever made. Opening hours: 09:00- 19:00 Fri 09:00- 11:00; 1:30- 19:00 Ticket Price(s): Regular: EP 60, Student: EP 30. Mummies Room: Regular: EP 100 Student: EP 60.

Since the museum contains more than a quarter of a million objects spanning over three millennia from the Old Kingdom to the Roman period, it would take at least nine months to see everything, and only if allowing a minute or less at each exhibit. That calculation doesn't include the vast number of artifacts languishing in the museum's basement. Some of the larger statues have reputedly sunk through the floor, earning the museum the ironic title of 'Egypt's last major excavation.' Cataloging is now, however, underway.

The ground floor is generally arranged chronologically (clockwise from the entrance hall), while exhibits on the first floor are grouped thematically. Tutankhamun's famous rooms are located on the first floor, as are the royal mummies and jewelry rooms.

The museum is ideally visited twice: once with a guide to point out the highlights (all contained in the main halls), and a second time alone wandering some of the side rooms, which give fascinating glimpses into the daily lives of the Ancient Egyptians. Guide rate: EP 50 per hour.

Luxor Temple and Statues

Luxor is a city on the east bank of the Nile River in southern Egypt. It is located at the site of the ancient city Thebes, known to be the Pharaoh's capital during the 16-11th centuries BC when the empire was at its peak. Today, Luxor surrounds two huge famous monuments: Luxor Temple and Karnak Temple. On the west bank of the River Nile are located the royal tombs of the Valley of the Kings and the Valley of the Queens. Essentially, the city is an open-air museum, which is the best place in Egypt to showcase its ancient past; the number of sights and monuments is too large, and it is difficult to finish visiting them in a short visit.

Luxor is an extraordinarily remarkable site with innumerable temples and tombs, each with its own story. The ancient Thebes city is mentioned as the greatest place during the reign of the Middle Kingdom and New Kingdom pharaohs who built huge structures for tombs, snugly hidden amid the rocky alley of Nile's West Bank. The magnificent structures of the Karnak Temple complex are only one example of the wonderful vista. The sheer huge number of monuments where tourists can simply soak up the elegance and grandeur can take a good part of the weeklong visit.

The temple complex of Karnak is considered to be an extraordinarily outstanding example of ancient Egyptian civilization at Luxor. The complex consists of the Great Temple of Amun, the Temple of Khons, the Festival Temple of Tuthmosis III, besides scores of other structures. The whole complex represents the architectural progress during the successive Egyptian kings who added to this great historical complex with traditional designs combining the cultural advancements made during the times of the New Kingdom.

The tourists find all the structures built here at a gigantic scale when they look up at the mighty columns and colossal statuary. Having witnessed the peak of Egyptian civilization, they stand with their imposing grandeur. The tourists will need half a day at the least to experience the golden era of ancient history.

It is possible to walk along the riverside Corniche road from downtown and reach Karnak, but most of the tourists prefer to take a taxi due to the heat. One can also find convenient shorter tours of the complex depending upon the time available.

The most prominent and popular feature of the Karnak is an avenue of human-headed sphinxes stretching over one and a half miles (3 km). This street connecting Karnak to Luxor is said to have been used during the annual Opet festivities. The construction of the avenue began during the times of the New Kingdom and is believed to have been completed during the dynasty rule of Netanebo I (380-362 BC). Ptolemaic Queen Cleopatra had it renovated in 51-30 BC. It was used later by the Romans. Among the recent exploration, 850 old sphinx have been found along a section of Sphinx street that was built by Amenhotep III (1390-1352 BC). In the annual Opet festival, people carried the statues of Amun and Mut and re-enacted their symbolic marriage. At the Luxor temple, Amun is believed to have been magically transformed into Min, the god of fertility.

As many as 1350 sphinx statues are believed to have lined

the avenue of human-headed sphinxes together with the chapels stocked with offerings. Queen Hatshepsut built six of these chapels (1479-1425 BC). Each of these chapels was supposed to ensure a precise function like cooling the oar of Amun or receiving the beauty of Amun.

Islamic Cairo

The narrow lanes of the capital's Islamic Cairo district are crammed with important historical monuments, most of them dating back to the Fatimid era. These make the area uniquely historic. Among the important mosques in this part of the city are Al-Hakim, Bay al-Sihayami, Qalawun complex, Khan el-Khalili shopping area, Midan Hussain, and Sayyidna al-Husain Mosques, Al-Azhar, Sultan Hassan, Rifyali, Ibn

Tulun, Mohammed Ali, and many more. There is Citadel built by the Muslim caliph during 1176-1183, he defeated the Crusaders. The Khan el-Khalili is the most visited Bazar by the tourists where every kind of souvenirs are sold. The visitors can see the coppersmiths and artisans in their tiny workshops and stalls working on their craft.

This shopping area is also home to many wonderful architectural examples of structures of the ancient Islamic empires. The tourists can explore a wealth of history.

There are many budget hotels and restaurants in this area, but it might be advisable to avoid taking meals. One needs to be careful of occasional pickpockets among the crowded shoppers. Modest attire is recommended for walking on foot; mosques also require the covering of the bare legs and shoulders, besides taking off shoes at the entrance.

Abu Simbel

Among the most prominent ancient sites of Egypt, Abu Simbel, a UNESCO World Heritage Site, is on the west bank of the Nile river. It was dismantled and rebuilt in the 1960s to save it from the rising Nile waters due to the construction of the high dam at Aswan. Built in 1244 BC, it comprises two temples carved into a mountainside. Four 21- meter tall statues of a seated pharaoh Ramesses II (1303-1213 BC) are at the entrance. A second smaller temple is believed to have been built for queen Nefertari which has two 10-meter tall statues at the front, one of the queen and four of the pharaoh.

Ramesses II, the most prominent of the pharaohs, whose statue adorns the Temple, was a warrior king who tried to expand his empire far up to Levant, modern-day Syria. Apart from waging war to expand Egyptian territory, he also built magnificent monuments and numerous temples in which he was worshipped in the image of different gods.

At the entrance of the Temple, the four seated pharaoh statues at the entrance show him wearing a short kilt, nemes headdress, double crown with a cobra, and a false beard. Several smaller statues near his legs represent the relatives of the pharaoh that include his wife Nefertari, his mother Mut-Tuy, and his children.

Moving the Temple from its original site to a high ground was a successful engineering feat that took five years with 3000 workers and cost about $ 42 million.

The interior of the temple stretches for about 64 meters into the mountain. It has been observed by some visitors that the first and second atriums inside the mountain are not as grand as the exterior of the Temple.

The biannual celebration of the Sun Festival is held to mark the highlight of the tourist season in Aswan. On the 22nd of February and October each year, the early rays of the sun enter the temple to illuminate the innermost sanctuary of the Temple. The festival begins before sunrise with the participation of musicians and dancers to celebrate not only the glory of Ramses II and Queen Nefertari but the technological and astronomical advancement of ancient Egyptians. Tourists in thousands come to visit these temples daily, either through the overnight train from Cairo or the twice-daily flight from the nearest city Aswan.

Abydos Temple

The temple of Osiris in the dusty town of Abydos is considered among the most fascinating artistic ancient treasures of ancient Egypt. With majestic tall columns and walls, the visitors are spellbound by the beautiful hieroglyphics and intricate paintings. The temple of Seti I at Abydos, also called the Great Temple of Abydos, is a grand heritage of ancient Egypt, though he himself is regarded as one of the lesser-known New Kingdom pharaohs.

Because of the reign of Ramesses II, arguably one of the greatest pharaohs, Seti I is a lesser-known pharaoh, but his rule was a milestone in Egypt's history as he brought back order to Egypt and established Egypt's sovereignty over its eastern neighbors (present-day Syria and Levant region) again.

Aswan

Located at the winding curves of the Nile, and in the backdrop of orange-hued dunes, Aswan is a tranquil town, known for the dam constructed over the Nile at this site. It is a good place to spend quiet time apart from strolling along the colorful streets of Nubian villages or riding on camel to the desert monastery of St. Simeon on the East Bank. Watching the lateen-sailed feluccas on the river over cups of tea in the riverboat restaurants is a good experience.

St. Catherine Monastery

The monastery of St. Catherine at the foot of Mount Sinai is considered to be one of the oldest monasteries in the world. It is here where Moses received the Ten Commandments. One would see an amazing collection of religious iconography, art, and manuscripts. A visit to this monastery can take most of the visitors up Mount Sinai to see sunrise and sunset. For a better view and an easy route to climb the famous Steps of Repentance, one can take the camel path.

Sharm El-Sheikh and Red Sea Coast

Sharm el-Sheikh is a resort town between the desert of the Sinai Peninsula and the Red Sea. It is known for its sheltered sandy beaches, clear waters, and coral reefs. Diverse marine life and hundreds of Red Sea coral reef sites make Sharm El Sheikh a magnet for divers and eco-tourists.

The coastal line is fringed by white-sand beaches and swaying palm trees. Amongst the top beaches are Naama Bay, Jolanda Reef (divers flock here to explore the remains of the Jolanda, an old Cypriot freighter ship that ran aground in 1980), Ras Um Sid Beach and Reef, Jackson Reef. The fish life and enchanting coral gardens are the main attraction. Sharm el-Sheikh has a large number of five-star hotels offering luxury lodging; prominent of them are Steignberger, Rixos Prium Seagate, Rixos Shar el-Sheikh, Sunrise Montemare Resort, Sunrise Arabian Beach, Le Royal Holiday, Four Seasons, Royal Savoy, La Branda Tower. The rates are flexible and vary according to the season and the size of the group.

Located 90 kilometers north of Sharm el-Sheikh, Dohab is regarded as the backpacker resort of Sinai and a good alternative to the usual travel package of Sharm el-Sheikh. The vast number of shoreline cafés and casual restaurants are lively places, while the shopping district near the highway has clusters of souvenir shops.

Between Egypt's mainland and the Sinai Peninsula lies the straits of Gubal. One of the ends of the Red Sea splits into two gulfs - Suez to the west and Aqaba to the east. The water here is shallower that has plenty of nutrient-rich currents flow that attracts a variety of marine life in all sizes and shapes. With shallow reefs and a large volume of shipping traffic passing through this area, the 19th and 20th centuries saw many accidents. Thus, the Gulf of Gubal is considered to be the best place for diving to explore the shipwrecks. Also best for scuba diving, this place attracts adventure tourists. The guides on boats of diving safari can offer the best site for diving, including discovering old shipwrecks and the WW II memorabilia. The most famous shipwreck in the Red Sea area is that of SS Thilstlegorm. The other famous wrecks in the same direction are SS Dunraven, SS Ulysses, and SS Rosalie Moller, within just three kilometers of each other.

Colored Canyon

The multi-layered and mineral-rich rock formations in the Sinai desert, nearly 210 miles from Cairo city, are a great attraction and can be visited only by a private vehicle. Tourists are picked up from Dahab, Sharm el-Sheikh, and Cairo.

These rock formations are believed to have been the result of ancient seawater receding from land in a process spanning millions of years. The water erosion left this wonderful landscape of deep walls of a canyon, reaching up to sixteen stories with spectacular colors and shapes in sandstone and limestone. In some places, the stone is incredibly smooth, making it appear soft and billowy.

Temple of Kom Ombo and Edfu

The river Nile provides wide varieties of boat trips from water-front restaurants to ride along with the historic places along the river. Most of these are from the Pharaonic era, including the Temple of Kom Ombo and Edfu on the route between Luxor and Aswan. The date-palm studded landscape along the river banks offers tranquil vistas.

All the big cruise boats have a stopover at the Temple of Kom

Ombo and Edfu's Temple of Horus. One can also have the experience of cruising by feluccas (the traditional lateen-sailed wooden boats) in which one can have an individual itinerary, though these feluccas may not offer the luxuries of big boats. There are frequent cruise boats from Aswan and Luxor, but feluccas can be chartered only from Aswan.

Kom Ombo ('Mound of Ombo' in native language) is an Egyptian town, 50 kilometers toward the north of Aswan, Upper Egypt. The temple here is unique as it is dedicated to two gods known as Sobek and Horus. Like other structures in the region, Kom Ombo's origin is stretched to the Pharaoh times. It was speculated that an older temple from the Middle Kingdom stood at this site. It became a military garrison close to the Egyptian border in the south and was called Nubt (City of Gold). The changing history of the town saw its name changes. While the Romans called it Ambo, Greeks renamed it Omboi. The temple was built over a long period of 100 years, mainly during the reign of Ptolemy VI Philomtor around the second century BC, and completed during the rule of Ptolemy XII Neos Dionysos in the first century BC. During Roman rule, the temple had more additions to it.

As mentioned above, the uniqueness of having two Egyptian gods in the temple: Sobek, the crocodile-headed, and Horus, the falcon-headed. Another intriguing feature of the temple is that Egyptians in ancient times believed that Sobek and Set were allies in the war against Horus. After the defeat of Set, his allies changed themselves into crocodiles so as to escape from the enemy, Horus. It means, therefore, that Sobek and Horus were enemies, but both found a place of honor at the Temple of Kom Ombo.

Cairo Bazaars

If one wishes to have a true flavor of the vibrancy and liveliness of the people in general, one will have this while visiting bazaars in Cairo. As a matter of fact, most of the traditional bazaars in other Arab countries also present the same scene. In Islamic Cairo, it is the bustling market in the old Khan el-Khalili bazaar that attracts travelers. In its labyrinth of alleyways, one finds authentic Egyptian souvenirs like jewelry, an extensive collection of papyrus, perfume, scarves, T-shirts, hookah pipes (nargilas), and spices.

The Khan El-Khalili bazaar offers a variety of handicraft shops, coffee houses, restaurants, and street food vendors. It's an open-air bazaar, always bustling with noise and shoppers. For those following religious routine, the Al Hussein Mosque in the bazaar is convenient for offering prayers.

As elsewhere, the shops in Khan El-Khalili demands good bargaining skill. One can safely assume that the prices are already marked up with relentless bombardment from the vendors. It would be safer to knock down the starting price of at least 20%. One need not hesitate to walk away as the last chip. Due to the crowd and noise, it may be advisable not to bring kids to the bazaar.

There are bus tours for busy travelers to visit Khan El-Khalili, operated by many companies. The common public transport is via the nearest Cairo Metro station 'Nan El-Shaaria, a mile northwest of the bazaar. Most stalls in Khan

El-Khalili open at 9:30 a.m. ad close at sunset, seven days a week.

Coptic Church

Before and after Islam's arrival, the orthodox Coptic Christianity has always maintained a strong presence in Cairo. The Coptic Church in the oldest part of the city is said to be older than many Islamic mosques in the area. The story relating to the origin of this church goes back to St. Mark, who is said to have introduced Christianity to Egypt, giving birth to the first African Christian church in Cairo. More of the rich history of the Coptic Church can be learned from the exhibits in the nearby Coptic Museum and the ninth-century Hanging Church, both housed within the ancient Babylonian fortress. This area also has the oldest mosque in Africa, the Mosque of Amr Ibn al-Alas, and Jewish site Ben Ezra Synagogue believed to be the place where the pharaoh's daughter found Moses floating in the basket.

Visit the Coptic Cairo has been described by all the visitors, irrespective of their faith, as memorable. It is full of history and contains exquisite mosaics and woodwork in ancient structures. The narrow alleys of Coptic Cairo are lined with street vendors selling souvenirs and a variety of goods.

The Salah El-Din Citadel is a prominent tourist site, 4 miles southeast of downtown Cairo. To avoid the delay and hassle of the heavy auto traffic in the congested area, one can hire a cab or take a bus tour to this place. The bus tours offered by many operators cost about $ 100 per person. The place is open daily, except Fridays, from 8 a.m. to 4 p.m. Entry to the Citadel is priced at EP 60 ($7), which covers entry to all the mosques and museums within the fortress. (Additional charge for using the restrooms.)

One of the most popular non-pyramid attractions in Cairo, the Salah El-Din Citadel, is a massive fortress and might take a whole day tour. Built in the late 1100s by Salah al-Din, the founder of the Ayyubid dynasty and one opposed to the Christian Crusades. Among the prominent attractions is the Mohamed Ali Mosque, besides two other mosques and museums, and the well-known Gawhara Palace, which was built by the army commander Mohamed Ali of the Ottoman empire, in memory of his last wife.

Step Pyramid (Pyramid of Djoser)

Sandwiched between Giza and Dahshur in Saqqara (southern Cairo) and surrounded by palm trees, this archaeological site houses the Step Pyramid of Djoser, Egypt's oldest stone pyramid. This is the world's first large-scale cut stone structure forming a centerpiece of a huge mortuary complex. Its origin is traced to the period of the Third Dynasty (2649 to 2575 BC) and is said to be built for the pharaoh Djoser by architect Imhotep. In its original design, it was built as a tomb and has attracted tourists for centuries.

Besides the popularly visited Step Pyramid, Saqqara also has several interesting sites, especially for explorers. These are also ancient tombs and smaller pyramids, many in a crumbling state. Many travelers had recommended wearing sneakers because of the sandy area.

There are package tours on a bus that one can avail of from Cairo, or take a taxi. The bus trip costs, on average, $100). It is open daily from 8 a.m. until 4 p.m. (or until 3 p.m. during the holy month of Ramadan). Entry to Saqqara costs EP 80 ($7) for adults and EP 40 for students (less than $5). It includes entry to the Step Pyramid of Djoser and the Imhotep Museum.

Shopping

Like the usual shopping experience in many other Arab countries, the prices in the shops are subject to bargain. With bargaining skills, one can save up to 25% on the price initially demanded in the shops, tourist travels, or for buying souvenirs. A bit of haggling is, therefore, a must while shopping.

The local markets, also called 'souks,' are among hundreds spread over the commercial districts. These attract shoppers in large numbers, especially the Khan El Khaleel bazaar, which is regarded as historically the most famous and popular and attracts tourists looking for the local shopping experience.

In around the Khan El-Khaleel bazaar and other local souks, one will find narrow lanes jutting from the main street where one can watch the craftsmen working on traditional jewelry, colored glass, copper, and brassware. This is the usual pattern of souks in other cities as well, like Port Said, Luxor, Aswan, and others. However, if the visitors explore the lanes and narrow streets of the bazaar, they will find small workshops producing wonderful jewelry, glass, copper, and brassware. In Cairo, another market, 'Tawfikeya' is also prominent, which remains open until the early morning hours and sells more variety of goods. Similarly, the Friday markets are also held at different places; the one near the Citadel is most visited by the shoppers after the Friday prayers.

Whether tourists or locals, while shopping, one has to learn to negotiate to get the best price. It is more important for tourists. In most of the Arab countries, bargaining is always regarded as the most useful art. The vendors also, at the same time, have mastered the art of selling their stuff at the maximum price they can manage.

The traditional Friday markets and other local markets are a good place to shop for second-hand items besides objects like birds, animals, and other products brought from all over Cairo and from other regions. In Alexandria, such a market is called the 'Attarine' Market, where antique items of a wide variety are available in the narrow lanes. In the Northern Sinai region, there are weekly markets that are held on Thursdays when many Bedouins from all over Sinai bring their handicraft goods. The prices of goods in these markets are lower than those at regular shops and bazaars.

Egypt offers a good variety of traditional handicraft items to visitors. These range from spices, perfumes, glasswork, canopic jars, cotton dresses, cartouche, chessboards, decorative boxes, and many more.

It is a common scene in the country where one would find locals enjoying tea and shisha outside the restaurants or coffee shops. The traditional hookah pipe is decorated with steel or brass fittings. The shisha, aromatic tobacco, is packaged in a clay pot. For the purpose of souvenirs, one might buy a miniature model of the hookah pipe.

Egyptians make chess or backgammon boards with beautiful designs out of hardwood inlaid with bones, ivory, or other elements.

Those interested in Mediterranean cuisine might buy high quality, and cheaper spices found almost in all markets.

Egypt is home to the best cotton in the world. One can get plenty of choices in cotton, from colorful dresses to innerwear. Gift shops and places around the tourist centers display them. Now one finds a lot of cheap imported cotton garments, but it would be wise to pick up an authentic Egyptian cotton dress.

Many tourists like to buy a cartouche. The jewelry shops can put your name on a cartouche in a matter of a few hours to make it a great souvenir for dear ones. One has to ensure that it is stamped with 925 for purity to avoid buying something which is not silver.

Although perfume bottles can also be bought in other prominent places like Dubai, the Egyptian perfume and scented oil is distinct. The country has the traditional art of producing perfumes in a variety of fragrances. Small bottles of fine perfume can make a good souvenir. These are not very expensive, either.

Another typical Egyptian souvenir is papyrus. It is a material similar to paper that was used in ancient Egypt for writing. It comes from the papyrus plant that grows in the Nile delta. The good souvenir shops can explain to you the paper-like surface was used in Egypt and show you beautiful artwork depicting ancient gods and scenes of daily life in ancient times.

Small glass sand bottles are also popular as souvenirs. The small bottles are filled with colored sand, and sometimes the sand is dyed to present them in vibrant colors. One could have one's name engraved or the date of one's visit as a souvenir. Egypt is also well known for hand blown glass craft to make plates, glasses, candle stands, and decorative items.

Souvenir shops also offer mini pyramids, which make good memorabilia. These do not cost more than a couple of dollars depending upon the size and the material these are made of. One could examine them before buying to make sure that they are Egyptian and not cheap imports.

One finds that shopping in Egypt is a distinct experience. Usually, pushy salesmen tend to get annoying. Many shops offer tea to potential buyers, but one is not obliged to make a purchase there. The annoying salesmen can better be ignored, though one cannot avoid being pressured to buy. One should be prepared for haggling over the price.

Some tourists are attracted to the Bedouins and their handicraft items. The main Bedouin handicraft is in the form of jewelry pieces. Bedouins are from the Sinai Peninsula, and the items they make there reflect life in Pharaonic times or Islamic or Nubian motifs.

Copper is among the many substances that the Egyptian workers are skillful at using. There is a whole area in Cairo called the "Nahaseen" where the craftsmen specialize in producing all sorts of copper products. Moreover, a wide range of copper and brass goods are sold in markets and stores all around Egypt. The products include Arabian coffeepots, trays, and hanging lamps.

Since Egyptian cotton is famous worldwide for being the best type, buying any cotton products would be a good choice. Many shops, found in touristic and local markets and in large shopping malls, sell pure cotton made shirts, trousers, and the famous traditional Galabeya, the Egyptian loose all-in-one robe. There are also nice colorful scarves, bed sheets, and bed covers sold almost everywhere.

Some believe that since ancient times, selling and buying goods in Egypt has always been a ritual where the aim is not only haggling to get a lower price, but an affair in which the seller and the buyer would bargain so both of them would be happy at the very end. The seller or the owner of the shop would traditionally invite the tourists for a cup of tea or coffee while turning the place upside down to show off his products in the best manner possible. However, tourists should not feel obliged to buy something until they find an item they really like.

One of the best bargaining practices in Egypt, and maybe in many markets in other countries, is that when you find an item that really interests you, especially if it's an expensive product, you offer the seller half the price set by the seller. Of course, the shop owner will not accept half the price and will stick to his full price, telling the tourists how expensive and good his products are and sometimes he would lower the price a little bit. The tourist, on the other hand, should actually do the same with a price slightly higher. Afterward, it is always a good idea to walk away, which often causes the vendor to invite you back and offer dramatically lowered products.

Being in Egypt

Climate

Climate is one of the major factors you should consider when visiting Egypt. For those who come from Europe and America, there is some adjusting to do in terms of climate. If you are from the cold regions, you should preferably visit Egypt during the cod months. During the hot months, Egypt can be unbearable, especially to those who are used to cold climates.

Climate also brings along some serious technicalities. For instance, if you are visiting a warm country like Egypt, you should be ready to deal with sunburns. You are also likely to be exposed to developing country diseases such as typhoid and hepatitis. Thankfully, Egypt is one of the few African countries where you can visit without worrying about malaria or dengue fever.

Egypt has a hot season and a cold season. The period May-September is hot, and the cold season lasts from November till March. These can change slightly depending upon the winds blowing from the north. At the coast, temperatures tend to remain cooler but more consistent, ranging from 14° to 37° Celsius (57° to 99° Fahrenheit).

The temperatures in the desert fluctuate dramatically, reaching as high as 45.6° Celsius (114° Fahrenheit) during the day and dipping as low as 5.6° Celsius (42° Fahrenheit) at night. In the winter, the desert temperature has been known to fall as low as freezing during the night.

The best time to visit Egypt is either in March-April or in October-November. These periods allow moderate temperatures, fewer crowds, and better hotel rates, though some might not like to put up with high day temperatures during this period. Since winter is rated as the most popular time for Egypt to visit when the evenings are cool and breezy, there is a rush of tourists that sends hotel tariff and the cost of tourism-related facilities high because of tourist crowds.

Culture: Life in Cairo

The heavily populated city of Cairo has a high density where the presence of people is obvious everywhere. Like other Islamic countries, Egypt enjoys a high birth rate. However, as one of the most advanced countries culturally, academically, and socially, the country presents a representative way of life in the Arab world. Cairo, of course, with its huge population, is the microcosm of the country.

Life in Cairo, as in other major cities, runs at its own pace, crowded markets, noisy scenes in shops or in streets, shouting by merchants, wayward traffic, and braying livestock. The city has its own orderly pace that has been going on for centuries, and Egyptians, proud of their culture and traditions, are comfortable with it. It is for the foreigners, short-term travelers, in particular, to enjoy their visit in the historical context instead of the Western standard.

A large number of people speak English or French in addition to Arabic. People are cooperative and very communicative, trying to strike up a conversation with anyone. They're chatty and considerate to the travelers if they ask for direction to any place or want to shop. One might often be accosted with unsolicited offers of services of tour guides which can be ignored in favor of known guides from companies. One has to be careful of the scammers and vigilant for a possible loss of purse or wallet.

In all the Islamic countries in the Arab world, the atmosphere during the months of Ramadan is unique with religious fervor with loud calls to prayers, abstinence from eating and drinking during the day, living a pious life, shortened working hours, gaiety after the breaking of fast in the evening (Iftar) and more activity thereafter.

Due to the increasing traffic and less than a strict way of driving, the first time traveler might be taken aback by the chaotic traffic, slow and easy moving. With nearly 12 million population in the city, the ever-growing auto traffic has worsened. It grows tougher during the rush hour or during the frequent traffic jams.

Using the metro train or taxi will be more efficient for the tourists. The metro fare is cheap, and its service is efficient.

The bus fares are also not expensive, though the bus rides can be tough in the rush hour when the presence of pickpockets can also be a problem. The tourist buses are not crowded, offer efficient rides between fixed destinations but are expensive. Taxis are more affordable and frequently operate, including those between the airport and the city center, a distance of about 13 miles. It might be kept in mind, however, that sweet-talking taxi drivers can also be good in conning the visitors. Knowing the place to be visited in advance will, therefore, be very helpful.

The routine urban life is no different from what one sees elsewhere: people commute to work and socialize on weekends and holidays. Like the large metropolis cities in developing countries, living in Cairo can make you feel that the economic pressures, overcrowding, traffic congestion, and pollution is making daily life a grind. The majority of the women take charge of the household chores. Outside the family, there is the usual network of people who provide essential services: the bawwab (doorman), the baqqal (grocer), and the makwagi (ironing person). They undertake all the miscellaneous work as a caretaker and runner of errands.

In the city, where the vast majority of people are teetotalers, the nightlife isn't always as rollicking as it might be in the

West. Cairo is a cosmopolitan metropolis with bars, cafes, cinemas, and galleries. Locals rarely eat dinner before 10 pm, and it's not unusual for the restaurants in the well-heeled areas of Mohandieen and Zamalet or in the major hotels to be buzzing until 1 or 2 am. Nightclubs are few and far between, but there are always a few such places, mostly attached to large hotels.

For most of the Egyptian males socializing outside the home takes place in cafes, where one can smoke a sheesha, drink tea, watch a football match, or play backgammon without alcohol or the company of women.

As is evident in other Arab countries, there is a growing difference between urban and rural lifestyles. The former following the modern trend, though at a pace which is in line with the traditional style of dresses, music, art, literature, and embracing foreign cuisine. The cosmopolitan Cairo has a good mix of tradition and modern trends. People dress up in both styles, though recently, more women have taken to wearing the hijab. Exposed to the French and British rule, the visitor can see the traces of their norms, especially in dressing up and social and business conduct.

The country has enjoyed remarkable political stability when compared to the neighboring countries. In recent times, the public uprising in 2011 was the important event that shook life in Cairo. Unlike other bloody uprisings, this one did not lead to significant violence. But during that upheaval also, the tourists were not much affected. It would be wise in any case to remain aloof from local politics and avoid visiting the disturbed areas, making a note of the exact location of one's place of stay and the streets connected to it.

The majority of the natives follow a conservative dressing style that is in line with the religious and social practices. Tourists should also avoid trendy dress and wear long pants or skirts and shirts that do not expose too much. Women traveling alone might be the target of unwanted attention if dressed up in scanty clothes. Covering the head while entering a place of worship is a must.

Cairo Traffic

Since Cairo is a densely populated city, not to mention all the tourists visiting the area can create a traffic nightmare at times. The driving culture on the road or in parking spots also reflects the casual approach of the people.

Driving in the city is stressful, though many tourists often remark that being a passenger is scarier than controlling the wheel where you can have some degree of control. One will observe that the Egyptian driers are impatient, as one would find in many Middle East countries. Western rules concerning 'right of way,' signaling, and use of mirrors do not apply. Lanes are disregarded, with sometimes as many as four cars, side by side in a two-lane street. Side mirrors are folded in to save space. Cars cut in front of one another regularly, honking most of the time to give confusing signals to others. Traffic lights are frequently ignored.

Parking on the streets is free, but the difficulty is in finding a slot. Egyptians are experts in parallel parking, squeezing into the most unlikely gaps. Double parking is illegal but common. Those doing so leave their emergency brake free and the car wheels aligned so that it can be pushed accordingly by a blocked car trying to come out.

Crossing the street as a pedestrian will also appear on the same pattern. Smooth sidewalks are practically non-existent. Pedestrian tourists will find the sidewalks rudely blocked by litter, parked cars, holes, pipes, and wires. Crossing a busy street poses another difficult challenge. Pedestrians are ignored by traffic. Assertion and even aggression are required; otherwise, waiting for cars to slow down can leave you by the side of the road indefinitely. If a group of Egyptians is crossing, watch them and join them to cross.

Cab drivers love to chat, especially with foreigners. Be careful how far you'd like to be engaged in such a conversation. At times, a cab driver might act as an unofficial tour guide, pointing out important buildings and monuments. During rush hours, it is usual for a cab driver to pick up other passengers on board or to be dropped off first. The fare meters on the cab usually do not show current rates, nor do people go by them; they know the fare. Foreigners are expected to pay more than the locals.

The experiences of some travelers and bloggers about the state of traffic in Cairo makes for interesting reading:

(i) The right of way. In the absence of strictness in traffic rules, one doesn't see 'the right of way' rule. In a crude sense, the bigger the size of the vehicle, the higher the priority it enjoys on the roads. Similarly, pedestrians use their own discretion in crossing a busy thoroughfare at their choice as to if they have the right of way, just as the cars jumping before your vehicle to fill a gap.

(ii) It takes time to learn avoiding the lanes in which traffic makes turn ahead or has slow traffic for any reason. Better keep to the side of such lanes and watch for the right moment to make your turn.

(iii) Cairo traffic does not believe in the 3-second rule – keep a 3-second distance between the vehicles. It is not the normal traffic flow, especially in a downtown city.

(iv). People do not like to leave any gap between the vehicles, especially in the slow-moving traffic. Everyone tries to rush in to fill any possible gap to show greater haste. One has, therefore, to be practical in such traffic.

(v) In an attempt to get into any gap between the vehicles, drivers try to butt in where there might be some opening for them. And it is accepted that any vehicle which appears sneaking in has the right of way. One would see fronts of the vehicles always looking for any chance to get ahead.

(vi) One can expect any vehicle in front of you might make a sudden stop or turn without safe indication. It is therefore prudent not to allow a big gap between the car in front but also not to be close enough to crash on it for the sudden stop or turn by it.

(vii) At the same time, driving in fast-moving traffic, one needs to keep as much gap between the vehicle in front of you to be ready to face a sudden erratic turn or behavior of the vehicle in front.

(viii) It is not only the sudden change in the behavior of the vehicle one is following, but one could come across unmarked speed bumps or potholes or the sudden appearance of any pedestrian whose possible intention needs to be understood well on time.

(ix) Pedestrians need safety in their jaywalking. There is no need to express your anger or frustration. Crossing in the middle of a busy intersection has to be tolerated and shown due courtesy if they happen to be elderly, women, or children, they deserve it.

(x) It is useful to be aware of the likely move of the pedestrians; some might stare into the eyes of the drivers, figuring out when the moving vehicle is going to slow down to give them the way or whether the vehicle has no intention to do that. There is a constant attempt to assess each other's intentions.

(xi) Most common and acceptable practice is to keep honking to ward off any possible accident. It is essential to make the presence of your vehicle known to everyone everywhere. Thus, most drivers on Egyptian roads don't have to look into their side mirrors and are, therefore, not expected to be aware of the vehicle following them. When in anger or frustration, one can give a loud and continuous honk to bring attention to the stumbling block or to unruly pedestrians.

Social Etiquette

As in other Muslim countries, Egyptians also practice the same etiquette that is traditional, like showing respect to the elders, dressing modestly, abstaining from public consumption of alcohol, etc. Other etiquettes are taking gifts when invited to somebody's home for meals, using the right hand to eat and greet, taking shoes off before entering the house. Politics is generally a divisive issue, and religion too touchy. It is better to avoid discussions on these, though Egyptians tend to talk freely.

Egyptians are warmly communicative and welcoming. One way to say "hello" is "salām 'alaykum." The appropriate response to that is "wa 'alaykum is salām." You can also say "welcome," which is "ahlan wa sahlan."

Following the traditionally conservative approach socially, Egyptians expect modesty in dressing up, whether for business or leisure. Egyptians are more progressive than many other conservative people in the Middle East, yet foreigners are expected to be modest in conduct and dressing up. But foreigners need not follow the Egyptian dress code, which might be considered a severe faux pas.

Public consumption of alcohol is frowned upon, especially in religious places, though many Egyptians exposed to the Western style enjoy alcoholic drinks. Alcohol consumption, even as a celebratory occasion, is not on. If offered drinks in private, one should still take them modestly.

Egyptians are very communicative at every level. They are fond of laughing about themselves or their country, though foreigners should not indulge in jokes or sarcasm about them. It will inevitably cause hurt to them, unless in special circumstances where it is acceptable by them to understand foreigners' views.

Tipping, 'bakhsheesh,' will be the most essential part of a traveler's experience; for those receiving the tips, the extra income supplements a wage that is often shocking by Western standards. Bakhsheesh is appreciated when small services are rendered, such as carrying bags and opening doors and to waiters and to anyone being extra helpful. Bakhsheesh is not reserved for tourists only. Egyptians tip at every opportunity and for the most basic of daily needs.

Foreigners are not expected to observe fast during Ramadan, but it is rude to eat or drink in the street while others are fasting. So, eating and drinking can be done indoors.

Old people are highly respected members of the community and are always given due courtesy. Egyptians are also courteous to others. If in public transport, there is a vacant seat, they invite others to take it rather than choosing to sit themselves.

As mentioned above, one will find a tendency among Egyptians to chat all-pervasive. They are free and express themselves openly. A traveler might come across someone even trying to improve his English, or a salesman or conman looking for a similar opportunity. One would do better just wave and smile and follow his way.

Bargaining is a special skill of Egyptians. There is no price fixed, every time one has to settle for a 'last price' that too after a great deal of haggling. The rule of thumb is to agree on a 'final price' that is 25 to 30 percent lower than the asking price.

Egyptian business people and also government officials, especially those who play the role of decision-makers, are more conservative than their counterparts in the West. The business executives are attired in suits and ties and not dressed up casually at the workplace. They appreciate conservatively well dressed up individuals right from shining shoes to a neat hairstyle.

Business meetings are normally conducted in a formal manner. Networking is the basic foundation of the business activity that might include someone playing the role of a go-between. Even if one is pressed for time, one has to have the patience in initiating or waiting for the business issue to come up for negotiation. They welcome to discuss specific arrangements, and if the business meeting ends without agreeing on the next agenda at the next round, it might just be the end of it.

In line with the strict conservative lifestyle, one will not find couples publicly demonstrating their amorous activities, cuddling or kissing in public, not even simple handholding. On the other hand, chatty Egyptians will not hesitate to be flirtatious with women travelers or voice their remarks on a woman's beauty. However, it doesn't go beyond that since a man touching a woman, if not married, is gravely frowned upon. In case a traveling woman finds it persistently annoying, she can assert and raise her voice to draw attention to the passersby – a deterrent for such elements.

While talking or touring, pointing one's finger can also be considered rude; one can show gestures with an open hand.

In their customs, shoes or flip flops should not be left upside down, a sign of bad luck. This is according to the ancient native superstition that upside-down shoe facing the gods will displease them. Seeing the shoes placed upside down might attract the attention of Egyptians who would offer to put them right.

Similarly, it is considered to cross your legs that might expose your shoe bottom to others. They wouldn't like to take even a photo of the shoes placed upside down.

Another common Egyptian courtesy not supposed to be acted upon. Such courtesies are called 'boatman invitation' because Egyptian generosity offers an invitation to a friend on the shore for tea on the boat under the safe presumption that nobody will actually swim to the boat for the cup of tea. In other words, 'boatman invitations' are meant to be a part of courtesy that is extended when the other person will most likely decline with equal courtesy.

At times a traveler might hear an Egyptian saying, " you do not have to buy or pay for this, "please stay for the night," or "have lunch or meals with us" that are another form of 'boatman invitation' and if accepted could cause embarrassment to everyone.

Hospitality

The Egyptians are warm and masters of hospitality. The guest is revered, more so if he is a foreigner. Invitation to dinner should, therefore, be accepted gracefully. If dining out with an Egyptian who insists on paying the bill, the guest should also insist on paying it. Most of the time, there will be a push and pull, and it is the person with the strongest will who finally pays. If paid for, it is polite to return the invitation at a later occasion.

It is accepted politeness to leave a bit of food on the plate after finishing the meal. This is recognition of the fact that one has been well fed and is not hungry anymore. Use of the right hand is a must since the left hand is supposed to be used for unclean actions. Those who are lefthanders might find the use of cutlery a good solution.

When invited to an Egyptian home:

-Remove shoes at the entrance

-Dress up well and conservatively; appearances are important

-Compliment the host on the house, décor, and anything

suitable

-Wait for the host or hostess to indicate your place to sit

-Taking a second helping amounts to sincere compliments of the guest

-In any case, expressing appreciation for the food is a common courtesy

-Putting additional salt in the food is not considered necessary

Egyptians enjoy taking meals in good company. They believe that eating together will improve their appetite besides their concern if the other person has been hungry and might not be saying so or hesitating. This might be better understood from the Egyptian proverbs, "He who eats on his own will choke on food," or "A happy morsel can satisfy the need of a hundred."

Family Beliefs

As per the customs and social traditions, the family is a significant unit in social life. In all social interactions and relationships, the family assumes the foundation. The individual role is subordinate to the family's, and, of course, the status of tribe or group, wherever it applies, is on the forefront. The family network is traditionally considered to be most important, which encourages nepotism and promotes the patronage of the family, which consists of both the nuclear family and the extended one.

Arab Honor

In all of the Arab countries, individual, family, or tribal honor plays a pivotal role. The sense of honor which everyone is proud of governs interpersonal relations. It demands and expects respect and esteem for the people as a matter of obligation and righteousness. The individual's honor is intricately entwined with every member of the family.

An average Arab greatly values his sense of honor. Travelers to Egypt will find a manifestation of this in the demonstration of friendliness and hospitality to one another. Respect for the friends and others demands deference to the elders, especially those in positions of power.

The word of honor has epical sanctity, and anyone going back on the word is considered a sign of dishonor for the individual and the family as a whole.

Social Class

In most of the conservative societies, social class or status determines one's access to power and position. It is usual for the Egyptians to follow suit. One will find three main classes: upper, middle, and lower. The social class assumes an important role in shaping up the future opportunities of the people. One's status is defined more by family status and less by wealth. Thus the family status influences the individual standing much more than the accumulation of wealth.

With this conservative background, one finds little or no social mobility.

Social Meetings

Here again, greetings are based on both the class and the tribe or group of the person. A safer practice to follow the lead provided by the person one has to meet. The normal shaking of hands among same-sex individuals is customary. These are always accompanied by direct eye contact and an emphatic smile.

Where a relationship already exists, kissing on one cheek and then the other while shaking hands among the same-sex people customarily follow.

Between men and women, the women initiate by extending a hand. If she doesn't, then the man should simply extend greetings by bowing his head.

Gift Etiquette

When invited to an Egyptian home for meals, it would be proper to take good chocolates, sweets, or pastries and give them to the hostess. Flowers or bouquets are offered for wedding occasions or during illness unless, of course, one is sure that these will be appreciated.

The gifts should be handed over with both hands if it's heavy, otherwise with the right hand.

Taking small gifts for the children will show affection to them.

The gifts are not immediately opened on presentation.

Business Etiquette and Protocol

Generally, Egyptians feel more comfortable in doing business with the people or the companies they know and respect. It is, therefore, useful to first cultivate personal or working relationship before embarking on business negotiations.

It thus follows that networking and cultivating acquaintances are important for doing business.

Egyptians are hospitable all the time and will offer tea or coffee at the first business or social meeting. Accepting this hospitality, whether one takes a sip or not, is a good gesture that is customarily expected.

Because of the general tendency to judge people by appearances first, it is important to be well dressed before meeting someone.

Holding direct eye contact in meetings implies honesty and sincerity. Egyptians might often show intense stares.

Like people in other Arab countries, Egyptians tend to get emotionally charged with hand gestures in excitement. Normally, they are soft, friendly, and gentle. Occasionally, they might raise the voice or pound the table more to demonstrate their point more forcefully.

The rule of thumb is to show deference to the senior-most person in the group who might also happen to be their spokesman. This is in line with the social customs where hierarchy and rank take high precedence.

Egyptians are comfortable with their laid back style, but when it comes to business, they are efficient and sharp. The following might, therefore, be useful to keep in mind when it comes to doing business with Egypt:

-Business meetings should be planned and fixed in advance.

-It would be wise to confirm it a week prior to the scheduled meeting.

-It might be useful to reconfirm it a day or two before the meeting.

-The business discussions are not held in a confidential manner; they are open and frank unless there is special confidentiality about it. Interruptions between the meetings are; therefore, normal sometimes dealing with other than the original issues if a new participant joins.

-Meetings with high-level government officials are, however, in line with western business practices, and such meetings are conducted with no disturbance.

-Out of courtesy and the need to create a friendly ambiance, there could be prolonged pleasantries regarding health, family, and general issues. If one has a fixed agenda and issues for discussion, it might be useful to send them in advance. English is widely spoken and understood, the formal communications should go with Arabic translation.

-Social interaction is as important as the core business issue because the Egyptians prefer to be comfortable before conducting business.

-Good personal and social interaction is more important for conducting long-term business.

-They follow the hierarchical practice in business practices as well. The final decision is made by the highest-ranking or senior-most person.

-Generally, business decisions follow a great deal of thought. It takes longer if the government decision is involved as the bureaucratic procedures tend to take more time.

-Even in the private sector involving major enterprises, the decision-making process is hampered by the traditional bureaucratic guidelines and consultations. More visits and interactions might become necessary to sort out normal issues.

-In line with the Egyptian regard for experience and age, it might be a good idea to include such people with impressive positions or titles on your team.

-Egyptians do not show negative reactions, but one should be prepared to face a fair amount of haggling. Seldom is an initial offer regarded as final.

-Egyptians are quite forthcoming and direct and do not like to offer negative reactions, but if no response is received from them, then it should be taken as 'no.'

-Egyptians are gentle and suave and would not like high-pressure tactics.

-They are sharp and thorough in examining any business proposition. These should, therefore, be well documented and supported by facts or research.

-Like the business people in other Arab countries, Egyptians can also be tough negotiators.

-Dressing up well is important; the Egyptian counterparts will be attired in formal dress.

-Conservative business suits in a dark shade, lightweight, is preferable.

-Women need to be dressed appropriately, covering the head. Skirts and dresses should cover the knee with long sleeves.

-Men should not wear visible jewelry on the face or neck.

-Business cards should be bilingual, with Arabic text on the back.

-At the initial meeting, exchanging cards is a formal ritual.

-These should be handled properly for the Egyptian party to read it. Also, read the cards from the other parties before putting them in the card case or pocket.

Important Travel Advice

Do's and Don'ts

Nothing should be placed on the top of a copy of the Qur'an.

Tell your cab driver that you're an atheist.

Honor shown to Egyptians is appreciated and recommended.

People usually do not hold hands here and there, and kissing, hugging, and that kind of thing is definitely a no-no in Egypt. Some women won't even shake hands with men they aren't related to.

Refrain from commenting on political or religious issues.

Be prepared to chat. Egyptians are very talkative.

What to Pack

Now that you have an idea of what Egypt looks like, you probably have an idea of what you should pack. When traveling to a new country, most people prefer packing all their personal essentials. On the other hand, some people prefer traveling and buying most items along the way. Since this book is geared towards budget travelers, I will strongly recommend packing as many items as possible.

With that said, the amount of essentials you pack also depends on the duration of your vacation. If you will be visiting Egypt for a two or three-day business meeting, you do not have to bother packing a full suitcase of toiletries. You may go a day or two without using toothpaste from your favorite brand.

The list of items you could pack is endless, but I will stick to the essentials for an Egypt-bound traveler. For items such as toiletries, I will recommend sticking to your usual arrangement. Just pack the way you would pack while visiting any other destination. This is because Egypt is a busting country, with shopping malls for all personal essentials, just like other countries. However, if you will be traveling to a far rural destination, you should ensure that you carry out shopping within the capital before venturing out. So, what exactly should you pack when visiting Egypt?

Based on the weather of the country, you should be very cautious when packing your clothing. Otherwise, you might be forced to purchase an entire set of clothing once you arrive at your destination. Some of the clothing you should pack include:

Loose pants and long skirts: High levels of heat in Egypt call for light clothing. The other factor to keep in mind is that the Egyptians dress in clothing covering the whole body. For ladies, it is recommended to have some loose pants or long dresses.

Although it is not mandatory for men to cover up, you should also pick some loose pants. If you are wearing shorts, pack ones that cover below the knees. When picking clothes for your journey, avoid synthetic materials, and stick to natural fibers and cotton clothing.

T-shirts and button-ups: You should pack plenty of loose T-shirts and button-up shirts. Due to the high heat, I find it relaxing to venture out in casual T-shirts rather than button-down full sleeves when I am in Egypt.

Walking Shoes: A tour of Egypt cannot be completed in a cab. If you are visiting the country in the sun, you should be ready to venture out to the deserts, where most historical sites are located. This means that you will have to do a lot of walking. Consequently, you will need comfortable walking shoes. Black shoes are the best option, given that the terrain can be quite dusty.

A wide-brimmed hat: The other essential clothing you will need is a wide-brimmed hat. This works for both men and women. The hat will help protect you from excessive dust and the scorching sun. If you don't pack one, you may be forced to purchase one in your host country at inflated costs.

Swimsuit: Egypt is not all about archeological sites and museums. There are plenty of interesting sites to visit. You may find the cruise down the Nile very entertaining, which often calls for some swimming. Once you settle in, you will understand why swimming is more fun than cruising. It can get very hot at times, all the way to 47 degrees Celsius or higher. With your swimsuit, you can jump in the water at any time and cool off.

High SPF sunscreen: While you will be required to have most parts of your body covered, there are some parts that will remain exposed to the scorching sun. Sunscreen will help protect the exposed areas such as your face.

Cash: Cash notes are the main medium of trade while in Egypt. You do not have to pack plenty of notes, but ensure that you have some cash with you when traveling to Egypt. You can change the cash at the airport and use it to purchase a few essentials before you get organized. While there are some entities that accept universal cards, such as Visa, Master Card, and American Express, most entities only accept cash.

Reusable water bottle: Reusable water bottles are very helpful in a hot country like Egypt. While you may be required to purchase bottled water, carrying your reusable bottle is environmentally friendly. Further, carrying your water from the hotel room when you are heading out to a far off destination is advisable since you may not come across water vendors along the way.

Hand sanitizer: I recommend carrying a hand sanitizer whenever you are out on a trip. I usually bring mine everywhere I go to avoid messing up my health. In Egypt, you will find your sanitizer handy, given that it is a dusty place. Of interest is the fact that you will have to sample plenty of street foods if you love trying new cuisines like myself. This is the reason why you should always have your sanitizer ready.

Type C (European) plug adapter: You will be required to charge your phone when you visit Egypt. Make sure you walk with a type C European style plug with two round prongs. Ensure that you carry yours to avoid having to purchase new ones at your destination.

Bug repellant: You should bring around some insect repellant, especially if you will be visiting the Nile River. Mosquitoes like wet and warm areas, an environment that is replicated by the Nile. Otherwise, you should be safe if you choose to stay within the capital without venturing too much outdoors.

Travel sickness medication: One thing you should never forget is your travel sickness medication. Whether you like it or not, your body will never feel comfortable in a new environment. Climate change, coupled with long hours of travel, will bring some fatigue. Carry your travel sickness medicine and take them as soon as you arrive at your destination.

Portable charger: Bring along a portable charger if you intend to venture far from the city. You might spend too much time in the car or your phone to retain its charge. Make sure you either have a portable charger or power bank to keep your phone on, no matter how long you have to travel.

Final Words

Egypt is an amazing vacation destination. I know you must already be interested in visiting this vast and varied land, or you would not have been interested in this book. Thank you for reading to the end.

I have been to Egypt many times since that first fateful, expensive trip. Every time I visit, I find new experiences. Even on my modest salary, the most expensive part of my trip is often the cost of the plane ticket itself. I look for deals and travel at the cheapest times.

As I said in the introduction, saving money is about being armed with knowledge. Once you are familiar with an area, you know where you can get the best deals and aren't locked into spending money at the tourist resorts (with their outrageous prices).

If you can plan the accommodations, food, and attractions you wish to experience on your trip, you can plan your budget well. Just because your funds are limited does not mean that your fun should be!

Common Phrases in Arabic

1. Arabic nouns are either masculine or feminine. Most feminine nouns end in the suffix 'a', 'or 'ya.' Only masculine nouns are used here.

2. There is no indefinite article, e.g., a, an. The definite article 'the' is 'il.'

Internet:

Is there a local internet cafe? Fee kafay internet hina?

I need internet access 'aayiz astakhdam il internet

Family:

My father - waldi

My mother - walditi

Dad - ba'ba

Mom - ma'ma

Wife - mirat

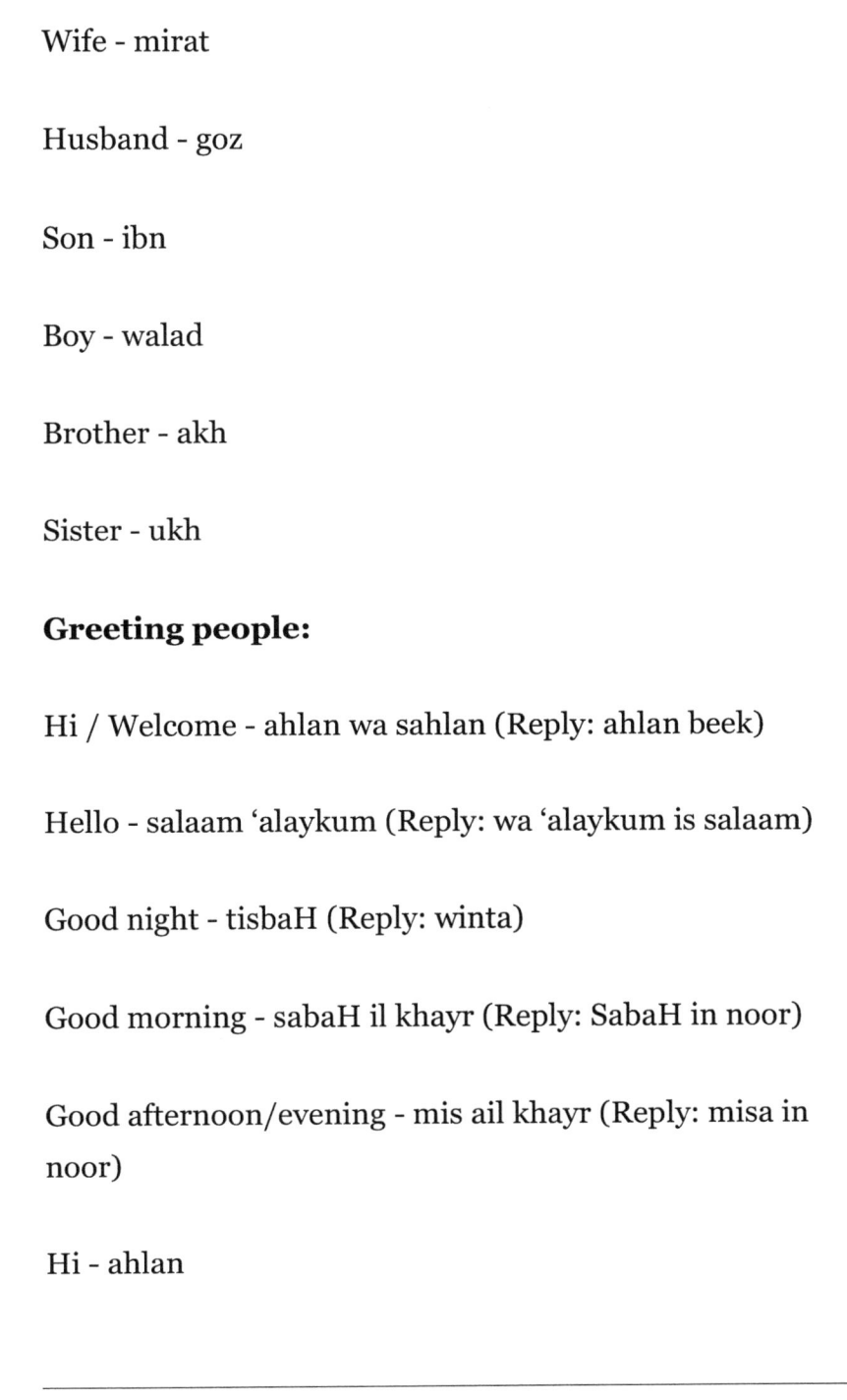

Husband - goz

Son - ibn

Boy - walad

Brother - akh

Sister - ukh

Greeting people:

Hi / Welcome - ahlan wa sahlan (Reply: ahlan beek)

Hello - salaam 'alaykum (Reply: wa 'alaykum is salaam)

Good night - tisbaH (Reply: winta)

Good morning - sabaH il khayr (Reply: SabaH in noor)

Good afternoon/evening - mis ail khayr (Reply: misa in noor)

Hi - ahlan

Goodbye - ma'is salaama

Bye - bai

How are you? - Izayyak (Reply: hamdulillah)

And you? - Wa inta?

How's it going? - 'aamil ey?

What is your name? - ismak ey? (Reply: ismee .....)

How old are you? - 'andak kam sana? (Reply: 'andi ....'years')

Are you married? - Ingta mitgawwiz?

May I introduce you to... - mumkin 'arrafak bi...

I'm pleased to meet you - gtasharrafna

It was nice meeting you - fursa sa'eeda

I am phrases:

I'm - ... ana ...

Grateful - mutshakkir

Happy - mabsoot

Hungry - ga'an

In a hurry - mista'gil

Sorry (apology) - aasif

Sorry (regret) - nadmaan

Well - bi khayr

Worried - al 'aan

Other common phrases:

Excuse me - an iznik

Sure - akeed

Just a minute - da ee'a waHida

OK - maashi

Listen - isma'

I'm ready - ana gaahiz

Let's go - yalla beena

See you later - ashufak ba'dayn

Good luck - Haz s'eed

Just a second - sanya waHida

Everybody - kulli naas

National - watani

Conversational phrases:

Do you speak English? - Bitistkallim ingileezi?

Do you understand? - Faahim?

I don't understand - ana faahim

Can you speak slowly? - Mumkin titkallim b ra'Ha?

Could you repeat that? - Mumkin ti ool taani?

Please write it down - mumkin tiktibuh?

How do you say ...? - Izzay a'ool ...?

What does …. Mean? - Ya'ni … ey?

Finding your way:

Where's the ….? - Fayn il …?

Bus station - mawif il utubees

Train station - maHatit il atr

Road to …(Aswan) - it tari li …. (Aswan)

Airplane / Boat / Bus / Train - tayyara / markib / utubees / atr

How do we get to ….? - nirooH … izzay?

Is it far / close by? - Hiyya urayyiba / ba'eeda

Can we walk there? - Mumkin nirooH mashee?

Other means of getting there? - Fee muswasla yaanya?

City / Street / Village - medina / shaari / qarya

Directions:

Turn - da ... hawid

Right / Left - yimeen / shimaal

To the right / left - ala il yimeen / shimaal

At the traffic light - 'and il isha'ra

Straight ahead - 'ala tool

Behind - wara

In front / opposite - uddaam / usad

Far / Near - ba'eed / urayib

Hear / There - hina / hinaak

North / South - shimaal / ganoob

East / West - shar / gharb

Taxi lingo:

Taxi - taksi

How much fare? - Bikram?

Please slow down - haddi is sur'a min fadlak

Please wait here - istanna hina, min fadlak

Stop at the corner - wa'if alal nazya

Stop here - wa'if hina.

Continue - khaleek maashi

Buying a ticket:

Where's the bus stop? - Fayn maHatit il utubees?

I like to book a seat to ... - 'aayiz at Hgiz tazkara li ...

One-way ticket/Return ticket - tazkarit zihaab / tazkartayan

1st class / 2nd class - daraga oola / daraga tanya

Sailing terms:

Captain - rayyis

Blanket - bataniyaa

Island - gizeera

Oars - migdaaf

Sail - shira'

How many people on the boat? - Haykoon fee kam nafar fil felooka?

What time do sail? - HanibHar imta?

What is daily charge? - Il yom bikram?

Does it include food? - Da shaamil il asl?

Do we need sleeping bags? - miHtageen sleebinbaagaat?

Accommodations:

Where is the hotel ...? - Fayn il ... fundu?

Cheapest / Good / Nearby - arkhas / kuwayyis / urayyib min hina

3-Star / 4-Star / 5-Star - talat nugoom/arba nugom / khamas nugoom

Could you write the address? - Mumkin tiktibee il' unwaan min fadlak?

Single room / double room - ghurfa li waaHid / ghurfa lil itnayn

How much for? - Bikam li .... ?

One night / a week / two persons - Layla waHida / usbu' / fardaytn

Restroom/Washroom - ghurfat alaistiraha

My name is ... - ismi ...

Can I pay by credit card? - Mumkin nidfa' bi kredit kard?

Do you have a double bed room? - 'andak ghurfa bi sirir muzdawag?

Air-conditioner/bathroom / shower - takyeef / hammam khas / mayya sukhna

May I see it? - Mumkin ashufha?

Any discount for children/students? - Fee takhfeed lil atfal / talba?

Sightseeing:

Do you have a local map? - andak kharita maHolliyy?

Do you have a guidebook in English? - Fee kitab irshaadi bil ingileezi?

What are main attractions? - Ay ahham il uzarat hina?

We only have one/two days - 'andina yom / yomeyn bas

Shopping:

I'm just looking - batfarrag bas

How much is this? - bikam da?

Do you have others? - fee taani?

I don't like it - mish 'agibni

I like to buy - 'aayiz ashtiri

Do you accept credit cards? - bitakhud kredit card?

Do I have a guarantee? - Mumkin aba'at ha barra?

I'd like to return this - aayiz aragga 'uh, low samaHt

It's faulty - mish shaghghaal

It's broken - huwa 'atlan

It's too expensive - da ghaali awi

Can you lower the price? - Mumkin tinazzil it taman?

Have something cheaper? - 'andak Haaga arkhas?

No more than ... - mish aktar min ...

Souvenirs:

Alabaster - marmar

Applique - khayyarmiyya

Basket - sabat/isbita

Brassware - naHaas

Carpets - sagageed

Handicraft - shughl yadawi

Jewelry - mugaw harat

Food:

Breakfast - fitar

Lunch - ghada

Dinner - 'asha

Meal - wagba

Days, Months, Numbers:

Monday - yom il itnayn

Tuesday - yom il talaat

Wednesday - yom il arba

Thursday - yom il khamees

Friday - yom il guma

Saturday - yom il sabt

Sunday - yom il Hadd

Yesterday - imbaariH

Tomorrow - bukra

January - yanayir

February - fibrayir

March - maaris

April - abreel

May - mayu

June - yoonyu

July - yoolyu

August - ughustus

September - sibtambir

October - uktoobir

November - nufembir

December - disembir

0 - sifr/zeero

1 - waaHid

2 - itnayn

3 - talaata

4 - arba'a

5 - khamsa

6 - sitta

7 - saba'a

8 - tamanya

9 - tis'a

10 - ashara

Bibliography

1. www.unmbeo.com/food-prices

2. www.britannica.com

3. www.cairoscene.com

4. www.kwintessential.co.uk

5. www.commisceo-global.com

6. www.history.com

7. www.insightguides.com

8. "Egypt: 2019 Annual Research: Key Highlights. World Travel & Tourism Council, 2019, www.wttc.org/-/media/files/reports/economic-impact-research/countries-2019/egypt2019.pdf.

9. "Egypt." The World Factbook, CIA www.cia.gov/library/publications/resources/the-world-factbook.

Milton Keynes UK
Ingram Content Group UK Ltd.
UKHW021122031224
452078UK00011B/994

9 798230 557227